Wild South's

LIVING TREASURES

of New Zealand

Wild South's
LIVING TREASURES
of New Zealand

ROD MORRIS *and* **PETER HAYDEN**

Foreword by
SIR DAVID ATTENBOROUGH

WILD SOUTH

HarperCollins*Publishers New Zealand*

Dedicated to the memory and spirit of Sir Charles Fleming
— scientist, visionary, storyteller —
and to all those who honour the past
and who work in the present
toward a better future.

Photographs
Cover: A male Archey's frog with eggs against a close-up of paua shell.
Half-title: A Pacific gecko feeds at night on *Xeronema* nectar.
Title: A pair of yellow-eyed penguins pause on an Otago clifftop at sunset.
Contents: A pair of kea ride thermals in the Remarkables.

First published 1995
HarperCollins*Publishers (New Zealand) Limited*
P.O. Box 1, Auckland

Copyright © Rod Morris and Peter Hayden 1995

Wild South is a trademark of Television New Zealand Ltd

ISBN 1 86950 185 3

Designed by Sally Hollis-Mcleod
Production by Derek Ward, Moscow Design
Printed by HarperCollins, Hong Kong

FOREWORD

TELEVISION DID NOT INVENT THE WILDLIFE DOCUMENTARY — but almost. Before television arrived, virtually the only place where you might see a documentary film of any kind whatever was in the cinema. But anyone going there in the hope of seeing something serious about animals or plants would have been very disappointed. With only one or two shining exceptions, the wildlife on view was limited to filmlets with jocular commentaries that were clearly considered by the management to be no more than make-weights in the evening's entertainment.

Then along came television. Right from its earliest days, it gave natural history programmes a prominent place in its schedules. Their popularity steadily grew. Network controllers and others who watch and worry about the size of television audiences began to discover that an increasing number of viewers enjoyed such documentaries. Nor was it only the dramatic big game animals of Africa that attracted substantial audiences. Small creatures — ants and spiders, frogs and hummingbirds — when filmed in close-up proved to be equally spectacular and popular.

As the demand for such programmes grew, so a new breed of naturalist came into existence — a kind who spent all their days not only observing the natural world in great detail, but who became extraordinarily expert and ingenious at recording what they discovered on film and videotape. As a result of their patience and expertise, the quality of natural history documentaries grew and grew. Today, people all over the world, who may have no pretensions as naturalists or scientists, and most of whom live far away from desert or rainforest, are better informed about the wildlife of this planet than ever before in history. Nor is their knowledge and expertise restricted to the big, the glamorous and the exotic. They have also become aware that in their own back yards or in the woodland just over the hill, live creatures of the greatest fascination.

Of no country is this more true than New Zealand. Rod Morris and Peter Hayden, together with their colleagues at TVNZ, have spent decades filming their country's wildlife. They do, however, have one huge and particular advantage. Because of the remarkable geological history of New Zealand, the majority of their subjects are found nowhere else on earth. Some of them are justly famous, some are among the rarest animals alive today, and some, though relatively numerous, are so secretive that few people ever see them. Here they are, in all their splendour and beauty, complexity and glory. Treasures indeed.

Sir David Attenborough C.B.E., F.R.S.

CONTENTS

INTRODUCTION

IN THE EARLY 1970S A PARTY OF NEW ZEALAND WILDLIFE SERVICE WORKERS led by Don Merton was camped in a small patch of forest high on the sheer walls of the Transit Valley beneath Mount Tutuko in Southern Fiordland. Its mission was to survey the remaining kakapo in Fiordland and therefore the sole survivors of that species on mainland New Zealand. Among the surveyors was Wildlife Service cadet Rod Morris, who on their last night decided to camp out near the display area or "bowl" of a male kakapo, where he would attempt to photograph the bird's booming display, something that had never been captured on film before.

In the early hours of the morning, having fallen asleep, Rod was woken by the wind, which was blowing an annoying branch across his face. The "branch" proved to be the gently waving wing of a kakapo that was dancing and displaying to him and his sleeping bag. Unfortunately Rod's camera was 50 metres away, set up beside the bird's bowl, but after slowly extricating himself from the confines of his bag, Rod was able to move quietly up the hill to the camera, accompanied by the dancing kakapo. The result was a unique series of photographs that have since been reproduced in many books, magazines and calendars. More importantly, they represent the beginning of an epic photographic pilgrimage that has taken Rod to all parts of New Zealand and most of its offshore islands in search of these often elusive living treasures.

If treasure means accumulated wealth, then we need look for it no further than the great flocks of sea birds that inhabit the New Zealand region. Our cities are puny affairs in comparison with the great conurbations created by the coming together of countless albatrosses, petrels and penguins on offshore islands each summer to breed. The lives of these birds are hard, and the rules of survival, although simple, are strict. The city of birds tolerates no deviancy. There is great beauty here, be it in the plumage of a mollymawk or the crested eye of a penguin. But there is also the brutal efficiency of predators such as leopard seals and skuas, and the pathos of a muttonbird chick awaiting the next meal that will never come.

The most beloved of our living treasures is the kiwi. Though its name denotes New Zealandness, the bird is rare, remote and unknown to most. When observed, however, kiwi reveal themselves as resourceful, strong and unique — fine qualities indeed for a national identity. The blue duck, falcon,

A northern Buller's mollymawk feeds at sea off Otago Heads.

kea and takahe share top "billing" with Ernest Lord Rutherford, Sir Apirana Ngata, Kate Shepherd and Sir Edmund Hillary on the currency of New Zealand. By giving our birds, plants and landscapes equal status with the nation's heroes, we are acknowledging the special nature of these islands and a strong connection with them.

An uncut diamond is easily overlooked. It becomes a thing of beauty which gleams and sparkles in the light only when it has been carefully cut and faceted. The process of crafting and shaping the life forms of New Zealand has taken more than 80 million years. The uncut jewel was a living fragment of the long extinct supercontinent of Gondwana. The cutting and faceting has been carried out during long isolation by natural calamity and an absence of continental predators. The polishing has been performed by more recent winged arrivals. The result is an extraordinary and eccentric society of animals and plants quite unlike any other on the planet.

Outlandish experiments in form and function were more likely to succeed here than anywhere. Giants arose among birds and insects that frequently took on the roles of the mammals on distant continents. All life was similarly crafted by the unique conditions that long persisted on the islands of New Zealand.

Dawn on Little Barrier Island is deafening. It follows an equally rowdy night. The forest of this island refuge is chaotic, noisy and vibrant, in stark contrast to the now often silent forest of mainland New Zealand. Much of the life found on offshore islands can now only exist in such safe areas, cleared of predators. Islands such as Little Barrier, Stephens, Middle Mercury and Snares are treasure houses for much that is precious and rare.

We treasure objects for their rarity, but rarity brings species to an evolutionary knife edge. On one side there is recovery and resurgence, on the other extinction. The black robin has provided the most famous and joyous recent recovery story, but the rescue of this bird from the very brink of extinction is by no means the only example of such deliverance among the plants and animals of New Zealand.

Extinction may occur with the freak suddenness of a storm that sends a lone kaka beak shrub cascading in a muddy slip into the valley below. Or it may come slowly and imperceptibly as forests retreat and habitat is lost. We will never again hear the unworldly shriek of a laughing owl. Both it and the forest it was known to inhabit are extinct.

We Kiwis are a peculiar lot. Although we enjoy recognition and the accolades of achievement from our own kind, we are most impressed when these come from overseas. Our achievements, be they in art, commerce, film making, netball or yachting, are not "properly"' crowned until they have been acknowledged by fans and experts from beyond these shores. Our natural heroes and world champions of evolution, such as tuatara, kiwi, weta and many others, are widely known internationally. For many years the experts have come — Attenborough, Bellamy, Durrell and all the others — to see for themselves and help us appreciate New Zealand's living treasures. The Natural History Unit of Television New Zealand has recently played a pivotal role in taking the stories of these treasures to over 50 countries. Black robins and black stilts have become as well known internationally as *Black Magic* and All Blacks.

Rod Morris and I were both recruited into the Natural History Unit by Michael Stedman and began work in the same week of January 1980. These were the earliest days of *Wild South* and a children's wildlife series, *Wildtrack*. Since then we have worked together and independently on literally hundreds of stories that have brought the nature of New Zealand to the people of New Zealand.

The 1980s saw a great burgeoning of interest in the wildlife of New Zealand. Bookshop shelves swelled with natural history titles, care for the environment began to be widely discussed and practised, and *Wild South* and *Wildtrack* continued to bring our living treasures into the nation's living rooms. I found it challenging and liberating to be meeting so much of our wildlife, often for the first time, on expeditions that took us to some of the remotest and least accessible parts of New Zealand.

A tuatara feeds on a common gecko, Stephens Island.

We have turned birds, reptiles, insects and the scientists who study them into actors. Experts and enthusiasts have given of their time and knowledge most generously to explain their work (in some cases a lifetime's involvement), which we have digested and, I hope, faithfully precised into the inevitably few minutes of television. I am most grateful to these people — they have changed my life and inspired me as a storyteller.

In *Living Treasures*, Rod and I have attempted to bring together many of the stories we have told during our years in television. If some of the scenes I describe seem to come straight out of a *Wild South* film, it is because a few of them do and a great deal more deserve to. Of course, a frightening number of the "old crew" of New Zealand's wildlife can be reproduced in neither film nor photograph — they have become extinct. We can, however, glimpse within the pages of this book the proud past they all once shared.

Since pulling away from its ancient Gondwanan port 85 million years ago, the wonderful evolutionary ship of New Zealand has sailed a long, hard voyage in a great southern ocean. The crew has done its best in the face of the many perils and calamities that have lashed their vessel along the way, but the voyage has taken its toll. Some animals and plants have been unable to endure the rigours of island life and have become extinct; many others have undergone dramatic changes in form and function. Yet others have flown or swum to the ships pitching decks to make a home there. Those ancient island mariners that survive are our living treasures.

THE SEA BIRD CAPITAL OF THE WORLD

CHAPTER ONE

WHAT WOULD AN EXTRATERRESTRIAL MAKE OF PLANET EARTH?   One curiosity that a visitor from outer space couldn't help but notice would be all the water. Water is an intergalactic rarity, but as the spacecraft swooped low across the Atlantic Ocean, then up over the Andes of southern Chile and on to the vast Pacific Ocean, the visitor would see that here it is in abundance.

On-board instruments would indicate that all life forms on this planet are aquatic in origin, and that water covers more than two-thirds of the planet's surface. Returning to report to the Intergalactic Council that commissioned the journey, our visitor might recommend the planet be named Water to reflect its salient characteristic.

Meanwhile, Planet Water thrives. Witness that great society of sea birds that centres its capital on Aotearoa New Zealand and its scatter of islands, big and small, that range from the balmy subtropics to the stormy subantarctic. Each island in this zone has its own population of sea birds which arrive each summer and use the land as a breeding platform. The bird species that depend on the sea for their livelihood are comparatively few in number, but among the 300 species of sea bird known to man there are some that exist in inconceivably large numbers. By surveying all these islands and all these birds, it is possible to identify two families that are the undisputed leading lights of the sea bird capital. One family is the tubenoses; the other is the penguins.

TUBENOSES: SOUTHERN OCEAN SPECIALISTS   Although known collectively as petrels, scientifically these birds belong to the order *Procellariiformes* (from Latin *procella*, storm). The families within this order are the albatrosses, storm petrels, diving petrels, petrels and shearwaters — birds of the vast and stormy southern ocean. The feature they all share is a bulbous, hooked bill and tubenose, a combination which on some species looks as if it was designed by a committee but is nevertheless their badge of sea bird distinction.

In depressions near the base of the tubenose there is an organ which excretes excess salt — very handy, given that everything these birds eat, drink or swim in is salty. The concentrated salt passes

A wandering albatross sits next to her large, fluffy-necked chick in the tussock in the Antipodes Islands. The nostrils which distinguish all tubenose sea birds are clearly visible on their large beaks.

via a duct to the tubenose, then flows forward along a groove between the bill plates to drip off the tip of the hooked bill, giving the birds permanently runny noses. Finally and most remarkably, within the tubenose is an organ for detecting odour — an attribute virtually unheard of among other birds.

We are infrequent visitors to the city of the petrel. Petrels inhabit the restless southern ocean that occupies virtually the entire planet surface between latitudes 30° south and 60° south. However, on board a ship many days from land in these parts, the tubenose family in its seaborne element may be revealed with a single scan of the binoculars. What is more, each branch of the family is likely to be represented in that one sweep of the pitching horizon.

Out to the left a wandering albatross rapidly closes the distance between itself and the ship. Without a wing beat it soars on giant 3 metre pinions into the wind, lifting to gain height before descending and accelerating along the wave tips until, deserted by momentum, it lifts and dives once more.

A flock of boldly chequered Cape pigeons dips and squabbles in the churning white water aft of the ship. These gregarious little petrels, like the albatross, are drawn to our presence by the prospect of scraps.

In the distance the dark shapes of thousands of sooty shearwaters proceed purposefully north-wards. They are not in the least attracted by the pitching and rolling ship. The mission of the sooties, perhaps the most abundant of all tubenoses in the southern ocean, is to complete a successful migration away from approaching winter to the northern Pacific Ocean, in particular the seas off Alaska and the Aleutian Islands, where they will spend the northern summer.

Suddenly flashes of light and dark draw our attention to the other side of the ship. A close-up view reveals a dozen or so tiny sea birds rising and falling and then appearing to walk on water. These are storm petrels and are indeed worthy of their petrel name (from Latin *Petrus*, Peter, i.e. St Peter's bird, one that appears to walk on the surface of the water). Their dangling feet then push off from the sea surface and once again they flit like oceanic butterflies away into the grey vastness of the Furious Fifties to the south of New Zealand.

At first there is no sign of the remaining member of the tubenose family, but then one explodes from the sea. It flies with rapid wing beats, like a large bumble bee, close to the water. It then disappears into one side of a wave and reappears out of the other. It takes a direct line, powering through both air and water. In the extraordinary flight pattern of this bird, the diving petrel, we see not only the ease with which some tubenoses inhabit both air and water but also how readily this petrel might relinquish its command of the air and fly only in water. The diving petrel seems to occupy the natural halfway point between the superbly designed airborne petrels and that other great family of sea birds, the penguins, which have completely given up the power of flight in air.

PENGUINS: FLIGHTLESS SEA BIRDS   Surprisingly, or maybe not, the penguins' closest relatives are thought to be the albatrosses and petrels. Like the tubenoses, the penguins' territory is the southern ocean, and again their capital is New Zealand with its islands and territories. Here 11 of the 18 known penguin species come ashore to lay eggs — that most inconvenient avian legacy for these most specialised of sea birds.

A penguin is a fish bird. As a sleek yellow-eyed penguin pauses on an Auckland Islands beach before departing for a day's fishing, it is the bird we notice rather than the fish. It uses its bill to attend to its sleek, dark coat. It gives its dense layer of flattened feathers the same care and attention for a day at sea as a nearby skua gives its feathers for a day in the air. Both birds complete their preening. The skua takes off, flying low over the beach in search of food. The penguin waddles Charlie Chaplin-like into the cool ocean, where it too begins to "fly" — in water.

The world's smallest penguin flits and darts among the waving fronds of chestnut-coloured bladder kelp that grow abundantly in the harbour of Wellington city, New Zealand's terrestrial capital. The wings of the little blue penguin, like those of all penguins, have become flippers that allow this water-borne bird to stall, bank and turn in the manner of its aerial cousins as it hunts small fish in the dappled light of the coastal sea forest. Its squat 1 kilogram body slowly descends as it swallows a small wrasse. It then suddenly disappears, ahead of a trail of bubbles. The fish bird's two weapons are the speed and manoeuvrability provided by its flipper-wings and the camouflage from the counter shading of its feather coat.

From above, the little hunter is an indistinct blue shape that blends into the gloom of the depths beneath. From below, its white belly and pale pink feet are barely distinguishable from the glare of the sparkling sea surface. The littlest penguin, like all penguins, is countershaded dark on its back and

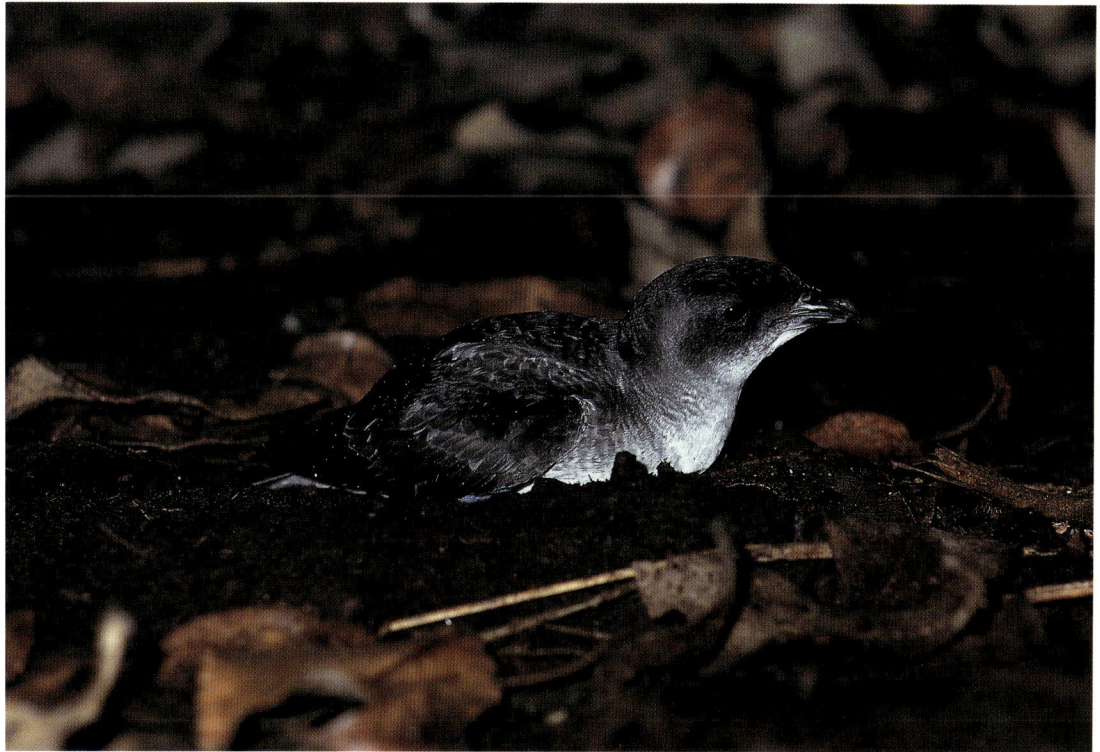

A diving petrel sits on the forest floor of the Snares Islands. This remarkable little sea bird shares characteristics with both the albatrosses and penguins. Its small, dense body, powered by short, strong wings, is sufficiently solid to fly unhindered through water as well as light enough to fly through the air.

white on its belly. The countershading even extends to its feet, which are spread out behind while swimming and act as rudders. It is the countershading of penguins that gives them their comical "little head waiter in a dinner suit" look.

The little blue penguin confines its hunting to the coastline of mainland New Zealand and southern Australia. Further south many islands of the sea bird capital support one or more of the several crested penguins. These are distinguished, above their flashing eyes, by a pair of yellow crests, which may be spiky punk, flowingly foppish or old-man bushy in character, depending on the species.

A group of erect-crested penguins, just back from hunting, porpoise magnificently along the smooth sea surface towards a desolate cluster of bare rock islets. They are heading unerringly for one of the larger of the 20 or so Bounty Islands. On this unusually calm day they have little trouble negotiating the skirt of bull kelp that gently swirls out from the sharp rock. They are ashore but not yet home. Home is above them, somewhere in the jumble of rock and amid the confusion of thousands of other penguins that are variously incubating, arguing or displaying. As if this wasn't enough, there are strangers among the penguins. The Bounties are one of the few places where the two first families of sea birds nest together in intimate contact. Between the two blended colonies of penguins and albatrosses there exists a community spirit which combines to oppose a mutual enemy — the skua. This predacious gull leers over virtually every penguin colony in the subantarctic, preying on eggs and small chicks. On the Bounty Islands, the tubenoses and the penguins must together repel the attacks of this rapacious hunter.

The great southern ocean and the ocean to the south around Antarctica is sea bird heaven. It is home to 10 of the 14 known species of albatross and most of the 18 species of penguin. They target the food-rich currents and upwellings that swirl out from Antarctica.

SEA BIRD CITY NIGHTLIFE   By late afternoon the low cloud has cleared around the Snares Islands. The southeasterly storm has moved away up the east coast of the South Island of New Zealand. The Snares are bathed in the soft light of dusk. A raft of Snares crested penguins preen and socialise offshore while being tossed about by the lively swell. Overhead the sky is steadily filling with the darting shapes of sooty shearwaters. It has been four months since their return from the northern Pacific. Most have partners sitting in burrows on the islands with newly hatched chicks, but all these "aerobats" continue to circle and dive, swoop and glide. As darkness falls there are perhaps three million sooty shearwaters in the air above the Snares, a chain of forested islands and rock stacks of no more than 300 hectares. Despite this small area, overhead and in the burrows are more sea birds than are to be found around the whole coast of Great Britain. The Snares Islands at dusk in summer offer one of the greatest wildlife spectacles in the world.

Without warning the sooties begin to drop through the canopy of trees. Once on the forest floor they pause to confirm their position before quickly making for their individual burrows, which they are perfectly able to find among all the others. Sooty shearwaters can alight within metres of home because they have spent the previous hour or so in the air plotting the position of their burrows using landmarks.

It is a bizarre night-time scene. The forest floor is alive. A procession of tubenose birds passes by two Snares crested penguins roosting on a low branch. To one side a male sea lion yawns and stretches in the ferns as a determined sooty shearwater attempts in vain to reach the safety of its burrow, which is concealed under one very large and unmoving flipper.

By 10.00 p.m. the storm that rocked the Snares Islands earlier that day has reached the town of Kaikoura on the east coast of the South Island. All the little blue penguins are back safely from the sea and are with partners and chicks in their burrows. However, fog and the storm have disoriented some Hutton's shearwaters. Perhaps a hundred of them sit blinking in the lights of oncoming cars, which slowly drive past to one side. An hour later, as the fog blows away to the north, they take off and climb up to the snowfields of the nearby Kaikoura mountains to seek the safety and comfort of their burrows. Here, as if in celebration of escaping near disaster, the colony is alive with their high-pitched chuckling calls throughout the rest of the night.

These days Hutton's shearwaters are one of the very few tubenoses to nest in the mountains of mainland New Zealand. They are certainly the only species to nest above the snow line; indeed, the snows may be ensuring their survival. It seems that many hills and mountains of New Zealand once boasted colonies of petrels, but predators, including cats, rats and mustelids, have finished their time there.

The little blue penguin is one of 11 species of penguin which live in the greater New Zealand region. It is the smallest flightless sea bird in the world, and is found round the entire coast of New Zealand.

Pioneer naturalist Edgar Stead, in his book *The Life Histories of New Zealand Birds*, brings together many accounts of petrels in mountains and hills from Fiordland to the Waitakeres, west of Auckland city. Stead says that of all the mainland petrels the most widespread was the mottled petrel. It was called the rainbird by early settlers, its distinctive call being always heard on rainy nights. The rainbird nested in several North Island locations, including Mt Taranaki, the Kaimanawas, the Ruahines and the volcanoes of the central plateau. In the South Island it was particularly plentiful in inland Canterbury. Stead's work indicates that the presence of Hutton's shearwaters at Kaikoura is no quirk of tubenose distribution, but a relic of a magnificent past when petrel burrows occupied hundreds, perhaps thousands, of hillsides on mainland New Zealand.

Throughout the short night on the Snares it has been as if each island has been conversing with itself. The forest floor murmurs. From millions of holes in the ground comes the sound of tubenose family life. An hour before dawn the noise increases and out of the burrows come the partners of last night's aerobats. It is their turn to leave the job of chick minding and to feed at sea.

Small processions of birds trickle along paths like mountain streams, meeting other streams to form rivers, which then converge with other rivers, all heading to the cliffs. Long before dawn has touched the eastern horizon, millions of sooty shearwaters have begun to take off from several major points around the island. By the time it is light enough to see, they are gone. All seems quiet now, but this is an illusion. It is only less noisy. Throughout the sooty take-off other sea birds have been beginning their new day.

The skies above Little Mangere Island in the Chathams group blacken after dark with as many as three million sooty shearwaters returning to their burrows.

As always, the Snares crested penguins going to sea this morning must run a biting, screeching gauntlet of home-stayers in order to escape their colony in a forest clearing. On another part of the island, in the shelter of the *Olearia* (daisy bush) forest, a colony of albatrosses with yellow stripes along the top of their tubenose bills gaze out sombrely from dark eyes with even darker shading around them. It has been a long wait. Some have been sitting on their eggs for 10 days awaiting the return of their partners — not unusual among southern Buller's mollymawks.

One female, however, has been waiting for 20 days, and that is too long. Her partner will never return. Two weeks ago he swooped on a squid that lay on the surface behind a large fishing vessel. That meal was his last. The hook hidden within the piece of squid bait lodged in the mollymawk's throat and the bird was pulled beneath the surface. He drowned as the 3,000 hook long line continued to be played out behind the vessel fishing for blue-fin tuna.

It is estimated that many thousands of albatross are killed on long lines each year. Albatrosses and mollymawks are scavengers and they will always be attracted to boats. Some albatross species with slow breeding rates have already suffered tragic losses. As the fish resource has declined, the number of fish hooks in the southern ocean has also declined, from 30 million each year to just a few million. But this fact does not help the female mollymawk that has remained faithful to the nest for 20 days. Finally, she rises above her warm egg and slowly walks to the cliff-top take-off point. She must feed today — if not, three albatrosses will die, not two.

New Zealand's sea birds range over a vast area, extending from the turbulent, food-rich seas of the southern ocean (*left*) to the warm, balmy skies of the tropical north (*above*), where this male red-tailed tropic bird hovers in flight. His black paddle-shaped feet and long, fine red tail plumes aid his acrobatic aerial manoeuvring during courtship.

19

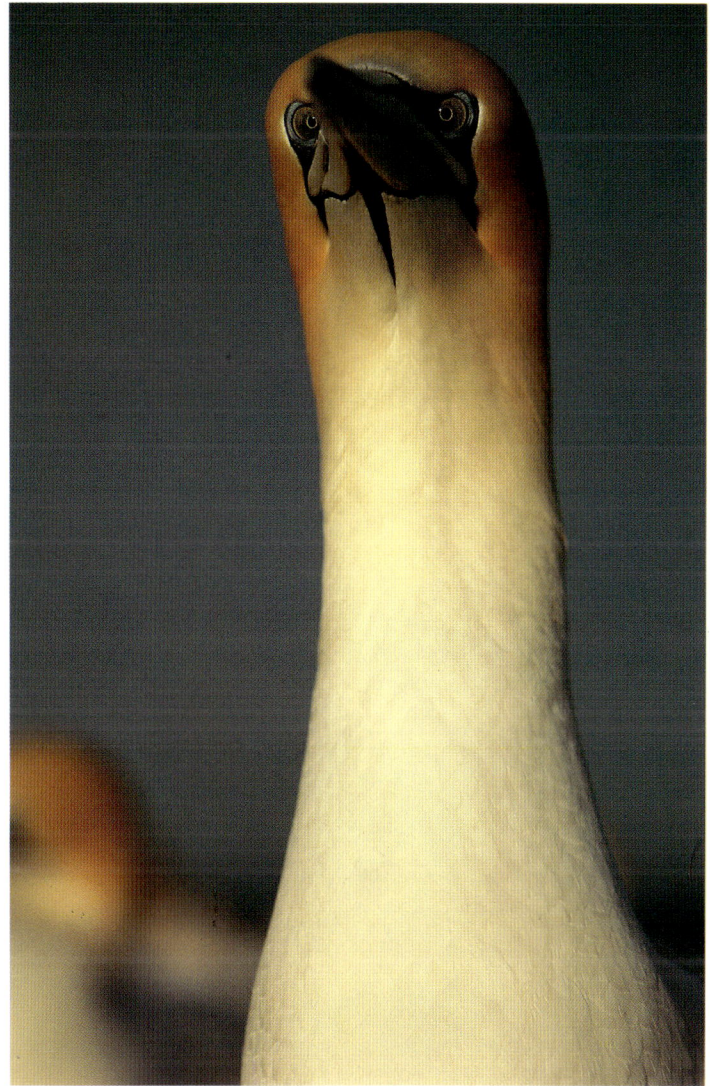

Left: Australasian gannets nest in serried ranks at Cape Kidnappers breeding colony, each nest just out of pecking distance from its neighbours.

Above: A male gannet looks down his nose at a neighbouring nest. Binocular vision enables gannets to determine distances precisely, be it the distance to a neighbour or the depth of food at sea, which must be accurately gauged before a gannet plummets to catch its prey.

Most of New Zealand's burrowing sea birds have now retreated from the mainland. These two South Island breeders are remarkable exceptions. The Westland
black petrel (*above*) still excavates its muddy burrows on the coastal foothills above
the farm paddocks near Punakaiki. The Hutton's shearwater (*right*) patiently awaits
the thawing of the snows above its icebound burrow high in the Seaward Kaikoura
mountains on the South Island's east coast.

Sexual attraction for many sea birds is only from the neck up. During courtship, the male spotted shag (*above*) possesses all the finery necessary for attracting a mate, from head crests and sparkling white filoplumes to turquoise facial caruncles and eye rings, but his adornments are temporary. Once he has acquired his mate the filoplumes fall out, the head crest wears thin and the colours round his eyes fade to an ordinary greyish green. Less foppish but just as transient are the bright blue eye rings, orange caruncles and red facial wattles of a handsome pair of Chatham Island shags (*right*). Following the prenuptial stage these birds, too, will revert to looking more ordinary.

Above: Looking like a distant field of daisies, a breeding colony of shy mollymawks covers the green slopes of Disappointment Island. Each "daisy" is a metre-high sea bird sitting atop its chimney-stack nest. Such vast sea bird colonies are a feature of many of New Zealand's subantarctic islands — tiny outposts of land which supply breeding platforms for the innumerable birds which feed and live in the vast southern ocean.

The bright red beaks of a pair of Caspian terns (*right*) and red-billed gulls (*above*) serve an important function during courtship; but they also serve as valuable advertising for the chicks when food is presented. Colour of a very different kind is important to the survival of both tern and gull chicks, including black-backed gull chicks (*top*). Here it is not so important to advertise presence as to conceal it. Camouflage plumage disguises these defenceless youngsters, as they wander around the colony or down to the wild shore, from keen-eyed predators.

There is nothing vague or uncertain about the courtship of a pair of Buller's mollymawks. The heavily mascara'd eyes, striking white eyelids and bold signal stripes down the beak are all designed to reinforce the exaggerated postures and gestures necessary to bring these sea birds into synchronicity for breeding. Such displays are always accompanied by loud, ecstatic gurgles and screams. Unlike the secretive courtship behaviour of our forest birds, courtship behaviour in a sea bird colony is overstated and ritualised and usually repeated again and again like any effective advertising campaign.

A lone royal albatross returns to its mainland breeding colony at Taiaroa Head, Otago. While many of New Zealand's sea birds now confine their breeding activities to offshore islands, the royal albatross is a magnificent exception, nesting near the outskirts of Dunedin city.

Above: A royal albatross feeds its eight-month-old chick, nearly as large as itself. Chicks being totally dependent on their parents for almost nine months, adult royal albatrosses can only breed successfully every other year.
Right: A pair of unemployed "teenage" albatrosses party at dusk at Taiaroa Head. The young male shows off in an ecstatic display. With head thrown back and wings outspread, he "sky calls" to impress his potential mate.
Far right: A three-month-old albatross chick, still covered in dense white down, sits unguarded on its nest while both parents are away at sea feeding. It could be two or three days before the next meal arrives.

A yellow-eyed penguin (*above*) perches partway up a cliff on the way home to its nest. As with other sea birds, beak, eye colour and crests are important features of courtship. The yellow-eyed penguin is the only penguin with yellow eyes, a characteristic strong enough to make it readily distinguishable even in bold close up (*right*).

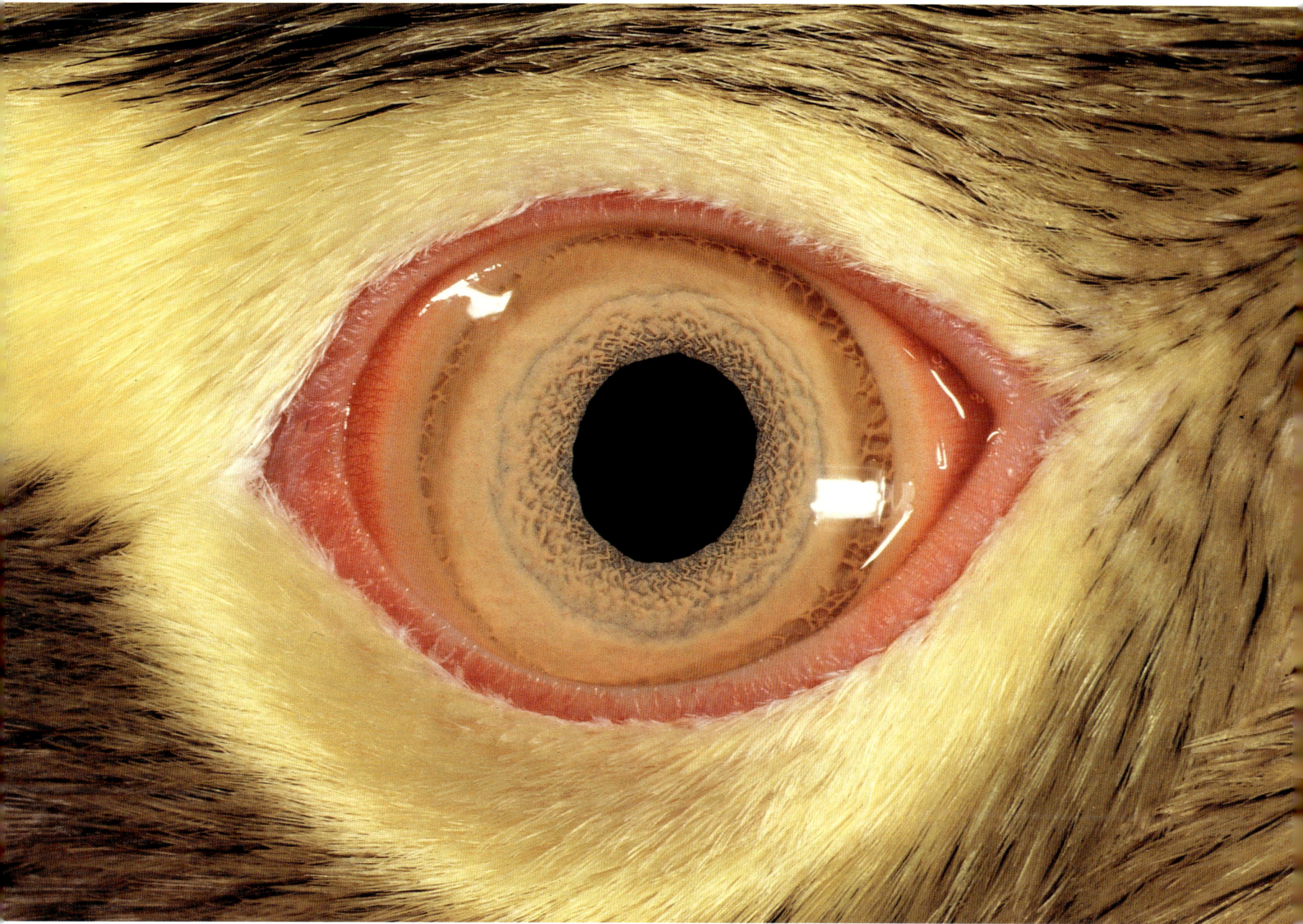

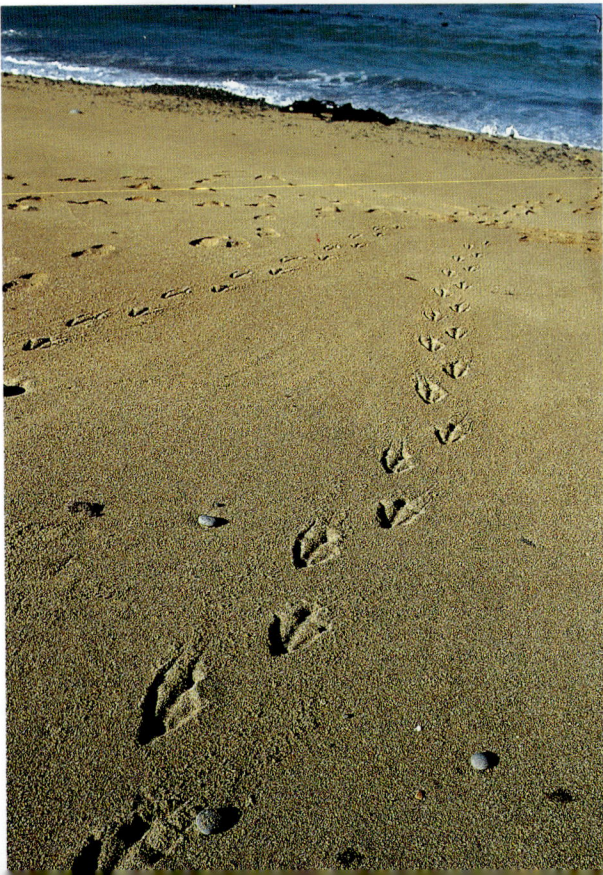

The early morning tracks of a yellow-eyed penguin (*left*) head purposefully down the golden sand on a South Island beach. The bird will spend all day at sea, returning just on dusk with its mate (*above*), to spend the night ashore. *Right*: In winter communal groups of yellow-eyed penguins may be found on wilder stretches of southern coast. Soon after stepping out of the cold water, their feet blush an uncharacteristic bright pink as circulation returns to the surface area of their skin.

Above: A little blue penguin (the world's smallest penguin species) balances on one leg to scratch behind her head, revealing two precious eggs in the nest. In a good season she will rear both chicks and may even renest before she retires to moult, having produced four times the number of chicks that a larger penguin is capable of producing.

Right: Down to the sea again. A small group of Snares crested penguins return to the water for a day's fishing, after a night in the breeding colony tending chicks.

All five of the world's crested penguins can be found visiting or breeding in the New Zealand region. The feisty little rockhopper (*left*), with its fiery red eyes and foppish crests, is readily distinguishable from the erect-crested penguin (*above*), with its brown eyes and vertical, brush-like crests. Both species often share the same colonies on the Antipodes Islands.

Right: Looking like some strange geological rock formation, rolled skins of penguins slaughtered in the distant past still lie preserved at the back of caves around crested penguin colonies. Such caches, left and forgotten, remain today a mute testament to the vast numbers of these birds that were once killed.

BIRDS CAN DO ANYTHING

CHAPTER TWO

Evolution on a large scale unfolds like much of human history, as a succession of dynasties.

Edward O. Wilson   HARVARD UNIVERSITY PROFESSOR AND ENTOMOLOGIST

...AND IN NEW ZEALAND THEY DID.   Following the extinction of the dinosaurs 65 million years ago, new dynasties arose all around the world. In New Zealand the new order was dominated by birds. They endured many natural calamities through the vastness of time, until the day that the first canoe furrowed a line up a forest-fringed beach and, later, an anchor was dropped in a sheltered bay. At both New Zealand landfalls, the sound of birdsong would have been deafening. What followed was the decline of birds and the rise of a new dynasty of mammals. Mammal power has reigned for little more than 1,000 years, but in that time 40 per cent of prehuman land birds have become extinct. Such has been the speed of change that if the birds had ruled not for 65 million years but for just 65 years (a reasonable reign for any monarch), then all we have done and undone would have taken place in less than half a day!

The one thing these birds that can do anything have been unable to do is endure the onslaught of mammals. Beak and talon have not been able to withstand tooth and claw. This led early observers to remark that the bird life of New Zealand was not only drab and somewhat boring in appearance, it was also degenerate and poorly adapted.

Little did such commentators understand the great dynasty that had existed here before. We must now view the rich bird fauna that inhabited New Zealand forests as we might view an Inca temple high on the slopes of the Andes mountains. We marvel at the ruined structure that remains, we imagine the great civilisation that once existed, and we are saddened that we can never know it.

A TOUGH SHIP   Prehuman New Zealand has been likened to a ship on a long and perilous voyage across the southern ocean. Along the way it nearly sank, its decks became covered with ice and then molten rock, the whole ship trembled and cracked with earthquakes, yet it survived and so did its crew — the

Rock drawings of moa demonstrate that these giant birds must have been familiar to the early Maori in New Zealand. Such drawings might provide us with fresh insight into moa behaviour.

birds. Some may have been aboard ever since the ship set sail from Gondwana 85 million years ago. Most others flew in later to make their home on this hulk of islands.

The dramatically changing landscape through time and space gave birds of many kind the opportunity to experiment with new lifestyles. Species radiated into new niches and took on specific roles. Change followed change, snuffing out some lifestyle experiments but initiating others. This was the New Zealand way of evolution.

At the same time the birds were shaking down into a fully fledged island crew. There were no mammals aboard to take on any of the big jobs, so the birds adapted to do it all. So successful were they that it is possible to look back and see among New Zealand's birds equivalents or analogues of the well-known mammals of the African savannah, the Amazon jungle and the European woodlands. Here in New Zealand were to be seen surrogate deer, rhino, monkeys, squirrels, moles, giraffes, mice and lions. In the dynasty of New Zealand wildlife, these roles were taken on by a remarkable cast of feathered opportunists. Many birds became flightless; some developed bizarre behaviour and habits. All were influenced in some way by this far-flung land such that they came to resemble the closest we have to creatures from another planet.

MOA MYSTERIES   The extinct moa were herbivores, or more accurately browsers of shrubs and trees, much like the deer of Europe, the bison of North America or the various antelope species of Africa. Though it is tempting to think of them as roaming in herds (or flocks) like their mammalian counterparts, moa were far more likely to have lived as individuals or in pairs and to have defended territories. Home, for most of them, was dense forest, where hearing and the sense of smell were probably far more important than eyesight. Did the greatly elongated trachea, or wind pipes, of some moa carry a bugle-like blast or a low-pitched boom over long distances? Some moa matters remain mysteries, but recent investigation of swamps, caves, dunes and other places where their pathetic relics have been found allows us to learn tantalising fragments of the story of these magnificent birds.

The last 2–3 million years of New Zealand's existence have been particularly turbulent. In that time, the Southern Alps have shuddered upwards and ages of ice have come and gone, dramatically lowering and raising both temperature and sea level. The geological ructions have also served to create more habitats, and perhaps more opportunities for moa. One thing is for certain — all 11 recognised moa species did not live together in the same region. By the best reckoning, seven species were found in the North Island and nine in the South. In any one tract of forest it would have been unusual to find more than three different moa, and even they would have been able to coexist only by specialising in eating different food.

Each time we try to picture how these shaggy-coated, big-footed browsers lived, we are left with the inventive limitations of our imaginations. However, recent reinterpretation of the significance of well-handled fossil bones and molecular analysis of moa fragments are solving some moa mysteries.

The most widespread moa was one of the smallest — *Anomalopteryx didiformis*, or the little bush moa. Part of the reason for this bird's success, through eons of change, was its strong bill and powerful jaw muscles. It could feed on tough vegetation at low levels in the forest. Towering above it in size but living in more open forest was the tallest bird in the world, *Dinornis maximus*. This, the giant moa, could reach high like a giraffe or deep into thickets to trim off a wide variety of leaves, seed heads and twigs. Its large body carried an enormous stomach that permitted long, slow fermentation of tough fibrous food that had been premasticated by up to 5 kilograms of rumbling gizzard stones.

Besides these and other forest dwellers there was one moa that stood apart. Initially it was considered to be like a huge kiwi (or apteryx), so was named *Megalapteryx didinus*. It browsed the mountainsides above the forest, on strong legs like those of a mountain goat. Its cover of hairy feathers extended right down to its feet. This upland moa performed much the same role as a mountain goat and contrasted most with *Pachyornis elephantopus*, a big, powerful flat-lander that was more like a hippopotamus.

For every single new discovery about moa there is another raft of questions to be answered. Did they scent-mark their territories? How did they care for their young? But each year brings forth new information, new facts that fire our imaginings, allowing us to dream more clearly about these "wonder-birds" that disappeared only a heartbeat ago in the life of these islands of feathered fascination.

WATTLEBIRDS   In addition to the moa, two of the original families of the bird dynasty were the wrens and the wattlebirds.

Three species of wattlebird survived through to European times, although only two are with us still. Between them they displayed a marked degree of variability of lifestyle within the forest. The distinguishing mark of wattlebirds, as this term suggests, is the facial feature of a pair of fleshy wattles (loose folds of skin) at the base of the bill.

At dawn kokako sing their haunting song from the tree tops of remnant stands of North Island podocarp forest. Pairs with territories that abut intone a slow, carefully rehearsed song cycle to announce their presence to each other and to the forest at large. Later, they glide down from their high perches to feed. As it glides, the kokako's short wings are splayed, giving it in silhouette the appearance of a sugar glider (or flying squirrel). Having landed, it looks even more like a squirrel as it runs along a branch and quickly ladders up to the next level. The bird runs and jumps through all levels of

Two New Zealand wattlebirds displaying different shaped beaks are the South Island saddleback (*right*), with a short, strong beak for chiselling open holes in rotten wood, and the female huia (*far right*), now extinct, which had a long, curved, probing beak for removing grubs and larvae from deeper holes and crevices.

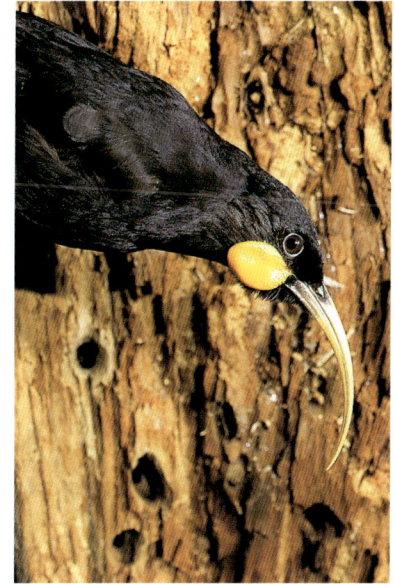

the forest, eating at least 30 different species of leaf, fruit and, occasionally, invertebrates. Standing on one leg and using the other as a hand to hold a tasty tawa berry and pass it to its mouth, a feeding kokako completes the picture of the mammalian arboreal herbivores, the monkeys and squirrels.

Wattlebirds are increasingly rare on mainland New Zealand, so to bring them all together we must roll back to a distant time when the dynasty of birds was at its peak.

A pair of *Euryapteryx* moa can be seen working over a coprosma bush laden with orange fruit. Nearby another bird with a bold chestnut patch over its black body attacks a rotten log with its sharp black beak. The force of the blows makes the bird's red wattles shake and wobble. This is a saddleback. Having paused to swallow a small flightless grasshopper, it is forced to scurry away due to the sudden arrival of a pair of larger bluish-black birds with white tips to their tail feathers. They, too, are recognisable as members of the ancient family of wattlebirds by the orange wattles at the base of their bills. And what magnificent and unusual bills they possess. The male huia attacks the log recently vacated by the saddleback. By plunging his dagger-like bill repeatedly into the log he makes the chips fly, excavating a convenient hole from which he extracts two plump huhu grubs. He hops away a short distance to digest them. Instantly his mate moves to the place he has vacated beside the log. She gently inserts her long, curved, ivory-coloured bill into the hole he has chiselled. Her head moves from side to side as she delicately probes like a surgeon deep into the interior of the log, from where she extracts several small insects. With her long, slender bill the female is more the anteater while he, using his bill like a jackhammer, is like a determined woodpecker. Having eaten their fill, the huia pair run and hop away into the deep shade of the forest.

No other bird in the world has shown such extreme difference in bill shape between male and female. Given the huia's broad dimorphism, who can guess what unknown species with other bizarre bill designs and lifestyles have disappeared through the procession of natural calamities that have befallen these islands during vast tracts of unrecorded time? Wattlebirds in New Zealand may once have existed in much greater diversity than the three known representatives.

A bellbird feeds on honeydew with its brush-like tongue. Bellbirds and other New Zealand honey-eaters, such as the tui and stitchbird, probably evolved from ancestors which flew here from Australia.

A FOREST OF OPPORTUNITIES   The old crew on board these islands have long received new recruits from across the ocean. All manner of birds, from ducks to predators, waders to songbirds, have been regularly flying to these shores. Many have survived by occupying niches that were available to them. In just the last 150 years New Zealand has provided a living for silver-eyes, white-fronted terns, spur-winged plovers, little egrets, Australasian harriers, shoveller ducks and others. Some species were successful colonisers at different times and became different birds.

As the tide recedes in a Northland mangrove estuary, a shy swamp bird with black and white barred markings and patches of chestnut and grey emerges cautiously to probe for marine invertebrates among the aerial roots. It and others of its kind have managed to colonise most remote islands of the southern and southwest Pacific. Ironically *Rallus phillipensis*, the banded rail, has achieved this momentous distribution despite being a reluctant flier, for when forced to become airborne it seems to be reluctant to land again and may fly a very great distance. In this strange way, banded rails have crossed mighty stretches of ocean to the west of Asia and Australia. When exhausted, they land on the water, and once they have recovered they take off again, like sea birds. A similar tale of trans-Tasman aviation can be told by another swamp bird nearby.

A few hundred metres inland from where the banded rail probes the mangroves, pasture reaches down to the edge of the estuary. Here a group of birds with red legs, bills and front plates, white bobbing tails and an iridescent blue sheen to their feathers can be seen rushing about. Two pukeko families are engaged in a lively dispute over which piece of lank pasture belongs to whom. They have the same argument every day. Pukeko are also rails or swamp hens, and like banded rails they appear awkward in flight but once airborne may travel great distances. Both these species stem from ancestors that arrived fairly recently on these shores. However, banded rails and pukeko have been making these epic flights from Australia for millions of years. The earliest migrants of both kinds have had time to change and adapt to their new circumstances. They left the swamp and entered the forest, where they seized new opportunities and took on new identities, thereby becoming unrecognisable from their ancestors. Both became fully fledged members of the feathered dynasty of New Zealand.

The takahe was once considered to be a giant rail confined to alpine regions, but we now know that two species once ranged widely through a variety of lowland and forest habitats in both the North and South Islands.

Island life can often have outlandish effects on species. Adults may grow up like overgrown chicks. The adult weka is big and flightless, like the chick of its ancestor, the banded rail. Weka are forest dwellers. They are intelligent and resourceful and have a highly developed sense of place — fine qualities indeed for newly nationalised citizens of the land of birds. Weka are both scavengers and predators, with a keen eye for anything remotely edible, from trampers' socks to mice, lizards to birds' eggs. Having lost the power of flight, they stalk the forest floor like feathered cats.

An ancient line of pukeko migrants has given rise to a forest dweller that became a browser like the moa. Takahe still have the colour of the pukeko but almost everything else has changed. Now they are rare inhabitants of a few Fiordland alpine valleys, but once they kept company with moa throughout the forests of New Zealand in both uplands and lowlands. In their restricted mountain home their substantial bills now pull tussock tillers or strip seed heads, but once they were used to snip and seize a great variety of forest foods. Takahe would also dig for fleshy underground roots and ensure their chicks had a well-rounded diet by giving them a regular tonic of forest invertebrates. Once a proud member of that highly esteemed group of forest herbivores, the takahe, having already given up its swamp, has now lost its forest and other lowland homes to predators and habitat destruction.

Weka and takahe were not the only swamp bird arrivals to take to the forest of New Zealand. There were others who came and changed even more radically into a highly specialised group with absolutely no interest in behaving like leaf-eating herbivores.

GUILD OF THE LONGBEAKS   The life of every leaf in a forest is limited. Most leaves are not eaten by a passing herbivore, but die on the branch and fall to the forest floor. The leaf litter on the forest floor attracts a host of fungi, bacteria, micromolluscs, insects, worms and other detritus-feeding invertebrates. All these wriggling, writhing or ramifying decomposers play an essential role in recycling forest nutrients and maintaining soil fertility. They are also an important food source for both mammals and birds, which target the decomposers in different ways. On continents, moles burrow blindly, following the scent of underground prey; birds do the same job without burrowing — they probe with long beaks.

45

New Zealand had no mammals until recently, so several shore and wading birds took to the probing way of life in the forests. Most were flightless and are now extinct, as their ground-based lifestyle was quickly eliminated when mammalian predators finally arrived. However, we know of these guild members from fossils and from living relatives that survive, out of harms way, on offshore islands.

The Snares Islands are one of the closest rat-free island groups to mainland New Zealand. As well as being a convenient breeding platform for several sea bird species, including penguins, shearwaters and albatrosses, they are also home to a number of land birds. The forest here is made up of daisy trees, and probing busily about in the leaf litter is a little bird, the colour of dead leaves, with stout legs and a long bill. It is the Snares Island snipe. Such a bird was once very common on the mainland. It is the smallest representative of the guild of the longbeaks. Its ancestors probably came from wetlands, and in New Zealand joined several other wading birds that changed to become longbeaks in the forest. Each species had a different-length beak and specialised in feeding at a different depth in the soil.

Thankfully the guild president survives — and it is right and proper that this leading figure among the longbeaks has the longest beak of all. It is of course the kiwi, the strange but steadfast national symbol of New Zealand. Some have suggested, rather unkindly, that a drab, flightless bird that uses its beak as a blind person uses a cane is an inappropriate symbol for a vigorous young nation. We, of course, know better. We know that the bill and many other of the kiwi's attributes and features make it unique. The four species of kiwi are quite simply like no other birds on earth.

At dusk a brown kiwi female emerges hungrily from her burrow at the base of an ancient totara tree. It is hardly surprising that she is hungry as she has just laid an egg that is almost one quarter of her body size (the equivalent of a 60 kilogram woman giving birth to a child close to school age).

The male brown kiwi, unlike the male of other kiwi species, incubates the giant egg on his own. If the female can get enough food, she will soon lay another egg for her mate to tend. She moves through the gloomy forest, tapping her long bill. This is not to avoid unseen obstacles but to find food. Kiwi are equipped with nostrils at the end of their long beaks. They are one of the few birds to make use of the sense of smell, often highly developed in mammals; but kiwi's use of this sense is not the only characteristic that inclines them towards "mammalness". The female's shaggy coat is more hair-like than feathery, and her body temperature is closer to that of the mole she imitates than that of her avian relatives.

By patiently probing rather like a mole with a periscope, she finally locates a subterranean burrow and sets about enlarging it. To do this her bill becomes a crowbar that wrenches the soft earth to form a funnel-like depression. Then it becomes a delicate set of forceps with which the female takes hold of the soft body of *Spenceriella gigantea*. With a steady yet firm pull she succeeds in bringing to the surface this giant earthworm, fully 1.3 metres in length and as thick as a finger. It is a meal indeed fit for a president.

The world's tallest bird, the giant moa (*Dinornis maximus*), seen here in a museum reconstruction, browsed trees to a height of over 3 metres. The 11 different species of greater and lesser moa would have exerted tremendous influence on the way New Zealand's plants evolved.

Top: The rifleman is one of only two survivors of a very ancient family of New Zealand wrens. A strong flier, it also hops and scrambles up the trunks and along the underside of branches of forest trees. Six other wren family members were not so fortunate. One partially flighted relative survives but the other five species, four of them totally flightless, were exterminated with the arrival of small mammals such as rats and mice.

Above: Other forest birds to have suffered include the New Zealand robin, a more recent arrival in this country than the rifleman. Its ancestors came here from Australia, and it spends more time on the forest floor than do its Australian cousins.

Right: A South Island fernbird returns to her nest. This secretive and shy bird is today confined to swamps and wetlands where rats cannot reach it. Once it would have ranged through scrub and forest margins.

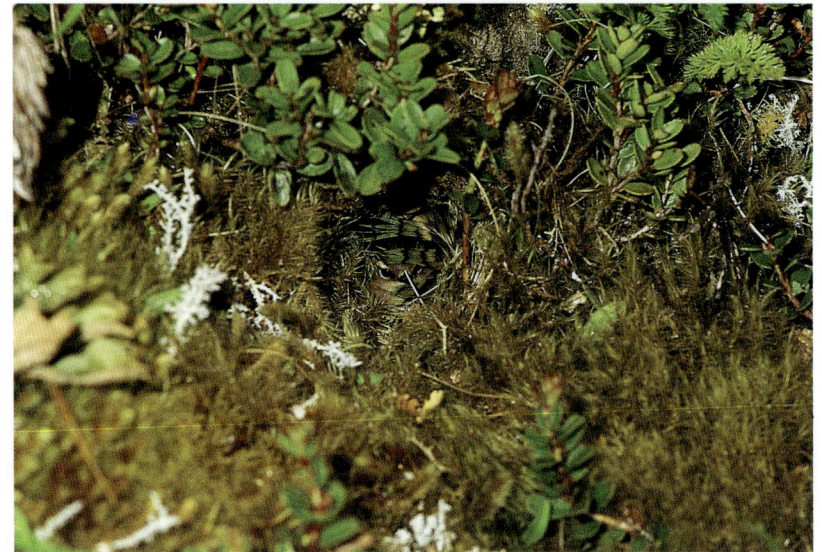

Above: A tiny rock wren discovers a kakapo feather nearly as large as herself and carries it back to her underground nest. Squeezing through her burrow entrance, she carefully places the feather inside her nest, where it functions as a camouflaged curtain through which she can peer at the outside world.

Right: A survivor of New Zealand's ancient wattlebird family, a North Island kokako gazes in interest at a pair of bright blue toadstools, *Entoloma hochstetteri*, growing on the forest floor. The bird's fascination with the blue fungi arises from the fact that they are the same colour as its own cobalt blue wattles, which are in turn important for courtship.

A western weka eyes up a dead native pigeon on the forest floor before scavenging it (*above*). This flightless "giant" rail is thought to have evolved from smaller flying versions similar to the banded rail (*right*).

Perhaps in the distant past a pukeko-like rail flew to New Zealand and gave rise over time to the giant, flightless takahe. The sage-green back of the takahe (*above right*) is a far more suitable camouflage for wandering head down through the tussock than the black back of the pukeko (*above left*).

Takahe Valley (*right*), where the takahe was rediscovered in 1948, is a remote alpine basin, buried under snow every winter. The takahe's large body size probably enables it to tolerate the low winter temperatures in the mountains, where it ekes out a living along stream and lake margins.

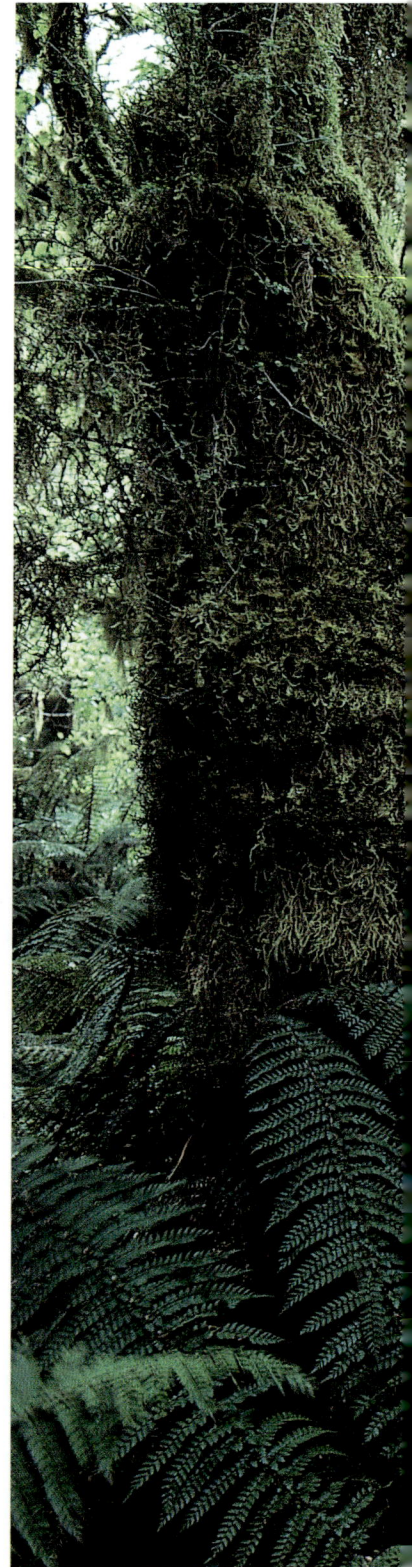

The black stilt (*above left*) is the only stilt in the world to have a solid black plumage, a characteristic shared with other "all blacks" such as the black oyster-catcher, the black fantail, the black tomtit and the black robin. Other waders, such as the Chatham Island snipe, seen here on a forest nest (*above right*), moved away from the shore and into the forest to exploit new food sources. In time the moist, dark forest (*right*) became home to a guild of long-beaked birds.

Above: A great spotted kiwi strides purposefully through West Coast rainforest, its long beak enabling it to probe deeply in the rich, moist forest soils for large earthworms.

Right: A little spotted kiwi gazes sleepily from its burrow. Its short beak enables it to probe for a variety of smaller invertebrates in shallow or drier soils. Once an inhabitant of the dryland mosaic forest on the east coast of the South Island, the little spotted is today our rarest kiwi and is no longer found on the mainland.

A North Island brown kiwi crosses a stream in a Hawke's Bay forest (*top left*). Kiwi have a highly developed sense of smell. Nostrils at the tip of their long beaks enable them to sniff out prey many inches below ground, as another brown kiwi demonstrates (*above right*).

Above left: A small population of an unusual form of the South Island brown kiwi, or tokoeka, holds out near Okarito. Some characteristics of these birds place them closer to the North Island brown than their tokoeka neighbours.

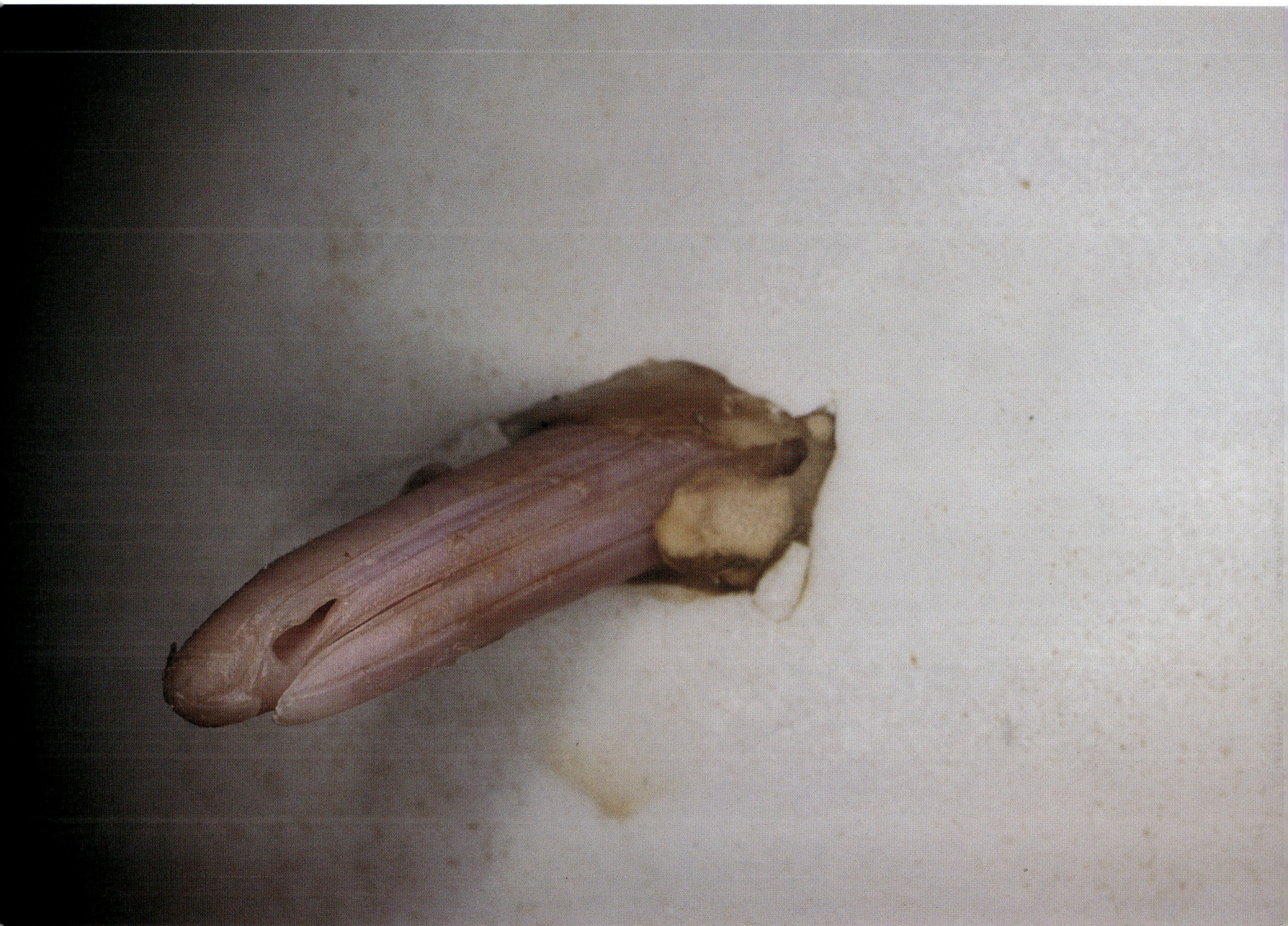

Left: The male North Island brown kiwi will incubate its enormous egg for more than 80 days before it hatches.
Top left: Oxygen deprivation is what causes the kiwi chick to crack the shell with its tiny, snorkel-like beak.
Above: The chick may remain at this late stage of development for a further 12 hours while it breathes in air for the first time and builds up strength for the final hatching.

Unlike most birds, a baby kiwi emerging from the shell is more reminiscent of a mammal being born than a bird hatching. Pushing with its feet and shoulders, it splits the weakened shell round the middle as a prelude to its birth. For the first two or three days after hatching, the young chick cannot stand up because its legs are spread so wide by the yoke sac still enclosed in its belly.

Remarkable as "ordinary" kiwi are, truly extraordinary individuals have been found on occasion, such as the three-legged great spotted kiwi (*above*) discovered in the Buller region. Most genetic mutations, as in this case, are disadvantageous and do little to aid a bird's survival, and after a prolonged period of illness this kiwi died. Other mutations are not quite as disadvantageous, as a white female North Island brown kiwi demonstrates (*right*). Nine months old and perfectly healthy, she lives on the island sanctuary of Little Barrier.

GHOSTS OF A LOST FOREST

CHAPTER THREE

IT IS A SOUND THAT SUDDENLY SILENCES ALL OTHERS IN THE PREDAWN FOREST.   The shriek, like that of a banshee warrior, is a warning. Sea birds in their burrows are mute, alert. The rasping tree weta and flightless click beetles have ceased their chorus. Bats, tuatara, even little spotted kiwi probing — all freeze. Silent wings bring the feathered angel of death to the forest floor. The faint scrunch of clawed feet on dry leaves charts its course through the gloomy forest. There is a lunge, a brief struggle, and then silence... Another shriek is heard. This time it is more distant and serves as an all clear. One by one the birds, reptiles, bats and insects of the forest resume their conversations and protestations as the first glow of dawn tints the sky beyond the limestone bluffs. Here a whekau, or laughing owl, drops a half-eaten tuatara and retires into a dry recess to rest.

By late morning the sun-drenched limestone is too bright to look at. Below, and about, there is the usual rye grass, number eight wire, hay barn, shelter belt, agricultural scene. The laughing owl and the forest of the night have disappeared. The wind remains. Balls of dry sheep dung are bowled at speed across the close-cropped pastures and down towards a large farm pond grazed to its muddy edge. When the forest was here, the pond was a swamp. A few such ponds, the limestone bluffs and the wind are all that is left of a unique forest type that once extended down the dry east side of New Zealand's South Island.

Journey far beyond the North Canterbury limestone bluff where the laughing owl once slept and you will find barely a trace of a lost landscape, known as east coast dryland mosaic forest. That it was dry is known from the climate of today. The nor'wester has blown hot and hard for many thousands of years. The mosaic or discontinuous patchwork of tall forest, shrubland and swamp was cut by thundering rivers. During surging floods that raged down from the Southern Alps, the rivers often redefined forest and riverbank. Within and around the mosaic forest lived animals in numbers and assemblages found nowhere else in New Zealand. We know all this from the methodical work of the many scientific detectives who are constantly analysing and interpreting the flora and fauna of the past. They

Perhaps the closest we will get to the vanished dryland mosaic forest of the past is in Frenchman's Gully, where cabbage trees and divaricating shrubs still cluster around the emergent limestone outcrops.

search eagerly for fossil bones, wood, pollen and other clues laid down in caves, swamps and other unlikely places. But the landscape itself also contains important clues as to who lived in the lost forest. The ghostly fingerprints of vanished animals have been left behind on the plants that remain. Many of the plants of the lost forest endure but have been driven into scattered isolation along the South Island's east coast.

The Seaward Kaikoura mountains are drained by powerful snow-fed rivers. On their way to the sea, these pass beneath steep bluffs that occasionally blush with cascades of flowers belonging to the pink tree broom. Only when in flower does this plant rate a second glance. A few tree brooms cling to the jagged rocks in an uncertain twilight between survival and extinction. The main reason for their perilous circumstance is that they are legumes, or nitrogen fixers, which renders them palatable to goats, sheep and other contemporary herbivores. They are also devastatingly susceptible to the sprays used to control introduced broom, gorse and other "modern" legumes. So here they must remain in splendid, craggy isolation among other far less imperilled shrubs. Among these are some strange plants that appear to have been turned inside out. Their leaves and some fruit are produced on the inside behind a barrier of half-dead, profusely branching twigs. This unfriendly habit, called "divarication", is far from rare. On the contrary it is to be found among 17 different families — or 10 per cent — of New Zealand's woody plant species. Inside out or divaricating plants were once a major component of the shrubland that fringed the trees, swamps and rivers of the lost forest. But why should so many different plants take on such an ugly aspect? The answer to this question could reveal the ghostly presence of New Zealand's large herbivores, the moa.

The prickliness of controversy surrounds this strange alliance of inside out plants. Some claim that it is the windy, unpredictable island climate of New Zealand that has brought forth close to 30 species of divaricating plant. Others say no. It is their counterclaim that the secateur-like beaks of moa have been the formative shapers of these plants. As moa lacked teeth, they would have fed by clamping, pulling and breaking off vegetation. A plant with tiny leaves, a highly branching and springy form and a rather tough exterior would have had little appeal. By contrast, deer, goats and other browsing mammals with teeth can easily nibble divaricating shrubs and so render the plants' defences useless. Mammals, which tend to have soft noses, are more deterred by thorns, and one reason why thorny shrubs are so rare in New Zealand is very probably because moa, with heavy, horny protection around their mouths, would not have been at all put off by such a defensive strategy.

The dryland mosaic forest was rich in plants of both the divaricating and non-divaricating type. Giant moa could reach up to three metres to take leaves, twigs and branches. In summer the profusely fruiting matai was a particular favourite. Even the smaller, more common eastern moa, *Emeus crassus*, with its weaker bill, would feed on matai fruit, along with the fruits and soft leaves of whatever else was seasonally available. It is likely that, like young takahe, moa chicks received an insect protein supplement to their otherwise vegetarian diet.

Much of our knowledge of the moa that browsed the lost forests of the South Island's east coast has been dredged up from the farm pond remnants of swamps. Pyramid Valley swamp in North Canterbury is famous for the great number of intact skeletons of birds that became mired there or were chased into the swamp over many thousands of years. Moa had to cope with numerous challenges, not the least of which were great alterations in climate over time. The vegetation in the valley of the swamp changed from ice age grassland to mixed forest following each of the bitter glacial periods. As climate and vegetation changed, so did the numbers and types of moa that came to the valley.

Following the end of the last ice age 10,000 years ago, forest quickly reclaimed most of the South Island. The year is around 160 A.D. A few years earlier, a great eruption in Lake Taupo destroyed much central North Island forest and the lives of many of the forest inhabitants. In the eastern South Island there has been no such calamity. On this day, a minor tragedy is being enacted in the swamp. The valley echoes to the piercing call of a giant moa. The large flightless bird is firmly stuck in the middle of a muddy swamp plain that surrounds what is left of the drought-shrunken pond. Already during the long hot summer several moa have become trapped in the mud on their way to drink. Unlike some of the others this one has little chance of escape. A massive eagle labours on 3 metre wings just above the helpless animal, which can only flail its long neck from side to side. Its cries take on an added tone of helpless defiance as the eagle grasps the moa's broad back in its great talons, forcing it into mud-soaked submission.

As death comes to the moa, the many other birds present around the swamp resume foraging, preening or otherwise occupying themselves, but each maintains a respectful distance from the feeding eagle. On the water several pelicans, together with an assortment of musk ducks, Finsch's ducks, pink-eared ducks and native swans, move quietly to the far side of the pond. Across the swamp a New

An Australasian harrier gazes fiercely at the photographer. Predatory birds were a powerful force in the evolution of other New Zealand birds, compelling many to become flightless, even nocturnal.

Zealand coot is shooed away from the nest of a giant rail. Several flightless geese wave their heads in gestures of mutual reassurance. A strange, stork-like, thick-billed bird called *Aptornis* resumes chiselling at a rotten log in its quest for an insect meal.

Of course, this ghostly scene can never be real. All these swampside spectators share the dubious distinction of now being extinct, like the forest that surrounds them. They share another dark secret, too. Over time, the same swamp that claimed the giant moa that day also preserved all their bones. Even bones of the great eagle, *Harpagornis*, have been found in the thick mud around the pond.

Harpagornis, the largest eagle the world has seen, became extinct around 500 years ago, along with its giant prey the moa. Not only has it left its bones in swamps and pit-fall caves, but its ghostly talons hang over living birds as vividly as if it stalked them still in the open spaces between patches of mosaic forest. Even within the shelter of the forest other birds were not safe. A large harrier hawk, three times the size of the recently arrived Australasian harrier, hunted among the trees, using its swept-back wings for greater manoeuvrability. Nothing escaped the powerful eyes of these two superior predators. They hunted throughout the dryland mosaic forest, scanning trees, shrubland, swamps and rivers for likely prey. The only limit on their predatory prowess was darkness. When night came, the eagle's and harrier's eyes became useless and their hunting patrols ended. This, surely, is a ghostly explanation as to why so many New Zealand birds abandoned the day and took to a nocturnal way of life.

Some birds played another survival card. They discarded the brightly coloured feathers of advertisement and put on the cryptic camouflage of the forest. A prime reason for kiwi, kakapo, kea and kaka to adopt one or both of these strategies of concealment was surely to hide from those eagle-eyed daytime lions of the sky. Does this also explain why some of New Zealand's cryptically coloured birds refound their bright colours in the centuries that followed the extinction of *Harpagornis*?

A lingering odour of formalin masks other, more subtle aromas that waft from the back rooms of one of our major museums. Past the shelves of stuffed animals from the African savannah, around by suits of chain mail and cupboards filled with Victorian collectables, eyes come to rest on several sets of drawers. One, labelled "*Strigops* and *Nestor* Colourmorphs", reveals a most unusual collection of stuffed parrots. Some specimens bear an uncanny resemblance to crestless cockatoos, others display an outlandishly vivid variety of colours. Upon closer inspection, and by reading the neat labels tied to each specimen's foot, they are recognised as bizarre forms of New Zealand's larger parrots. Study skins of orange-red and white kea, red and white kaka and golden kakapo lie in a cluster, as brightly coloured as autumn leaves. There is even a blue kakariki. More label reading reveals that the specimens were "collected" by several Victorian naturalists, for whom shooting and preserving was the acknowledged method of study. Is it possible that, in a few short years, naturalists with rifles selected out the colourful birds in the populations of parrots in much the same way as keen-eyed *Harpagornis* and the giant harrier had done centuries earlier? Will we, in years to come, see more colourful parrots now that Victorian naturalists have also become extinct? If nothing else, this is a colourful theory.

Even at night, most birds, bats, reptiles and insects of the lost forest did not have things all their own way. Others came out at dusk to work the predatory night shift. Of the three top nocturnal predators we still know two, while the third, and largest, has left us a ghostly inventory of its nightly attacks.

The first of these predators is the tuatara. Today we know it only from offshore islands, yet tuatara were once abundant in dryland mosaic forests. Their hunting technique of stand, wait and pounce can be effective if also rather non-selective. Tuatara are just as likely to clamp their jaws around one of their own kind as lunge at a giant weta. Perhaps this is why, as has been observed, statuesque adult tuatara come out at dusk and feed in the earlier part of the evening, whereas their darting, sprightly offspring tend to be active during the early morning.

The second nocturnal predator needs no introduction. At night it still regularly calls its name in many parts of New Zealand. It seems strange that in Maori its call is "ruru" while to English ears it sounds like "morepork". It is a small owl, from which no moth, bat, frog or small reptile is safe. Ruru's diet, like that of all owls, is well known because it ejects or vomits a pellet that comprises all the hard indigestible bits of its previous catch.

The final night-time predator is the one we can never know. The whekau, or laughing owl, has become extinct within historical time. Its shrieking laugh was heard early on dark nights or just before rain. Apart from its laugh it seems to have possessed either a great repertoire of different calls or merely a few calls which, like those of the ruru/morepork, have been translated in quite different ways. There is little doubt about the laughing owl's diet, however; from pellets left in many dry roosts it is possible to build up a shadowy picture of lost lives in dryland forest.

It is perhaps a rough kind of justice that tuatara, known to prey on its own kind, became prey to the laughing owl, which also hunted other predators including its fellow owl the morepork. The remains found by scientists at laughing owl roosts provide a virtual who's who of the smaller birds of the lost forest. On the laughing owl's menu were four different wrens, birds that behaved rather like feathered mice by gleaning tree trunks, leaves and leaf litter of insects. Bellbirds, tuis, robins and tomtits were also consumed in large numbers. Yellowheads, browncreepers and grey warblers were either less common victims or less favoured. Fantails were probably caught on their roosts or in their nests. Another favourite was the now extinct but once common piopio or New Zealand thrush. Being a ground feeder this bird was probably easily caught by the laughing owl, which frequently hunted on foot. Piopio may have been our sole representative of the great tropical family of bowerbirds.

The after-dinner remains of the now extinct laughing owl, full of beetle elytra (horny front wings), lizard skeletons and the bones of tiny birds, provide us with a picture of past inhabitants of the long-vanished dryland mosaic forest of the eastern South Island.

Laughing owls were no wimps. They stood almost 40 centimetres tall and were unafraid to hunt birds their own size or even larger. Kakapo, kiwi and pigeon all found their way into the stomachs of owls, as did the smaller kokako and saddleback. The South Island saddleback, found today only on offshore islands, still hides at night in fear of the ghostly laughing owl. Promptly at dusk it stops feeding and drops to a low, impenetrable roost, under a bank, in the centre of a fern or perhaps, as hut dwellers know, inside a ball of string or an old tin. This behaviour would have functioned well as protection against a predatory owl; but against the predatory mammals that came next to the dryland forests it proved disastrous. Finally, the bones of all three rat species appear in pellets of the laughing owl, shortly before this stalker of the night became extinct like the forest in which it lived.

The many ghosts of the east coast dryland mosaic forest remind us that it is quite untrue to say, as many have, that there were no predators in New Zealand before the arrival of mammals. Cats, dogs, rats and stoats are simply different predators, which use their noses to hunt. The birds, reptiles and insects of prehuman New Zealand were far from defenceless; they had spent millions of years fashioning the best defences they could against feathered predators that hunted by using their eyes. The wildlife of New Zealand was certainly not degenerate and already headed for extinction when humankind made landfall on these shores. As the ghosts of the lost forest show, they lived in an exciting, frightening, dynamic environment, and we are the poorer for never having known them or their domain.

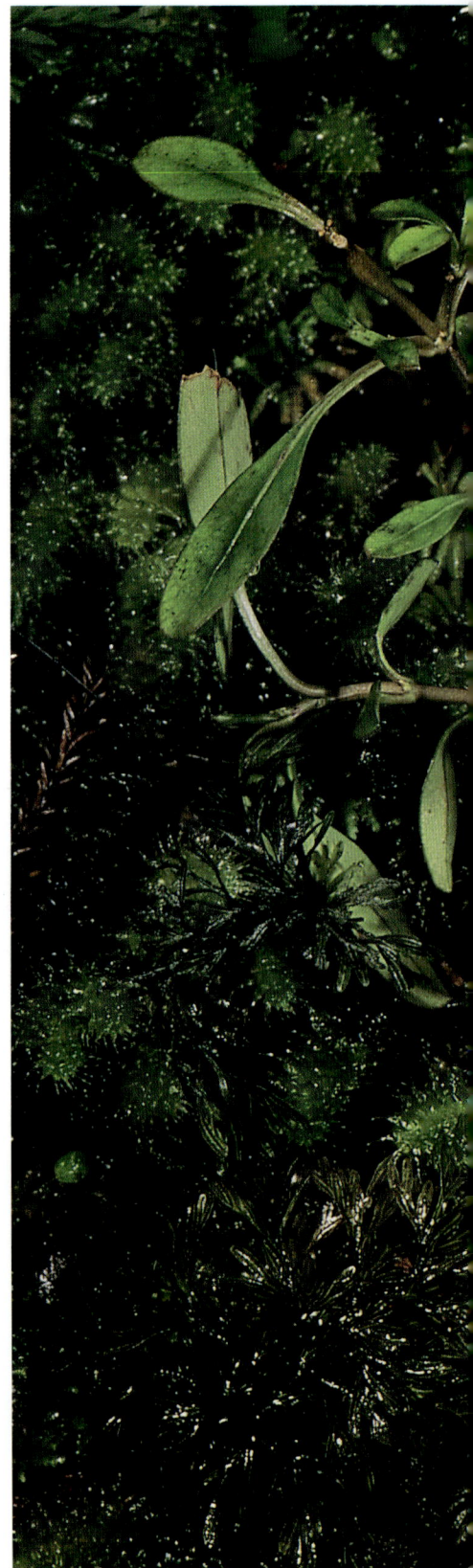

Quiet and retiring though the kakapo is (*above*), it still possesses many of the characteristics of the more typical members of the parrot family. It is both curious and playful — which can be gauged from the peeking eye of this male perched in a beech tree in the Sinbad Valley in Fiordland. However, a single feather lying on the forest floor (*right*) seems more at home amongst moss and leaves than it does on the body of a parrot.

All of New Zealand's native parrots bear modest colours when compared to the gaudy parrots of the tropics. Here a North Island kaka quietly preens its scarlet breast feathers (*above*). By hiding its finery under its wings and on its breast, the kaka escaped the attention of predators that hunted from the skies. With the disappearance of the giant eagle and the large native harrier, parrots in New Zealand began to express greater variation in all-over colour. Unfortunately these brightly coloured individuals were soon exterminated by Victorian collectors anxious to add them to their collections.
Below: The bright plumage of a red kaka. *Top right*: A white and a red kaka.
Bottom right: A collection including a canary-yellow kakapo and an apricot kea.

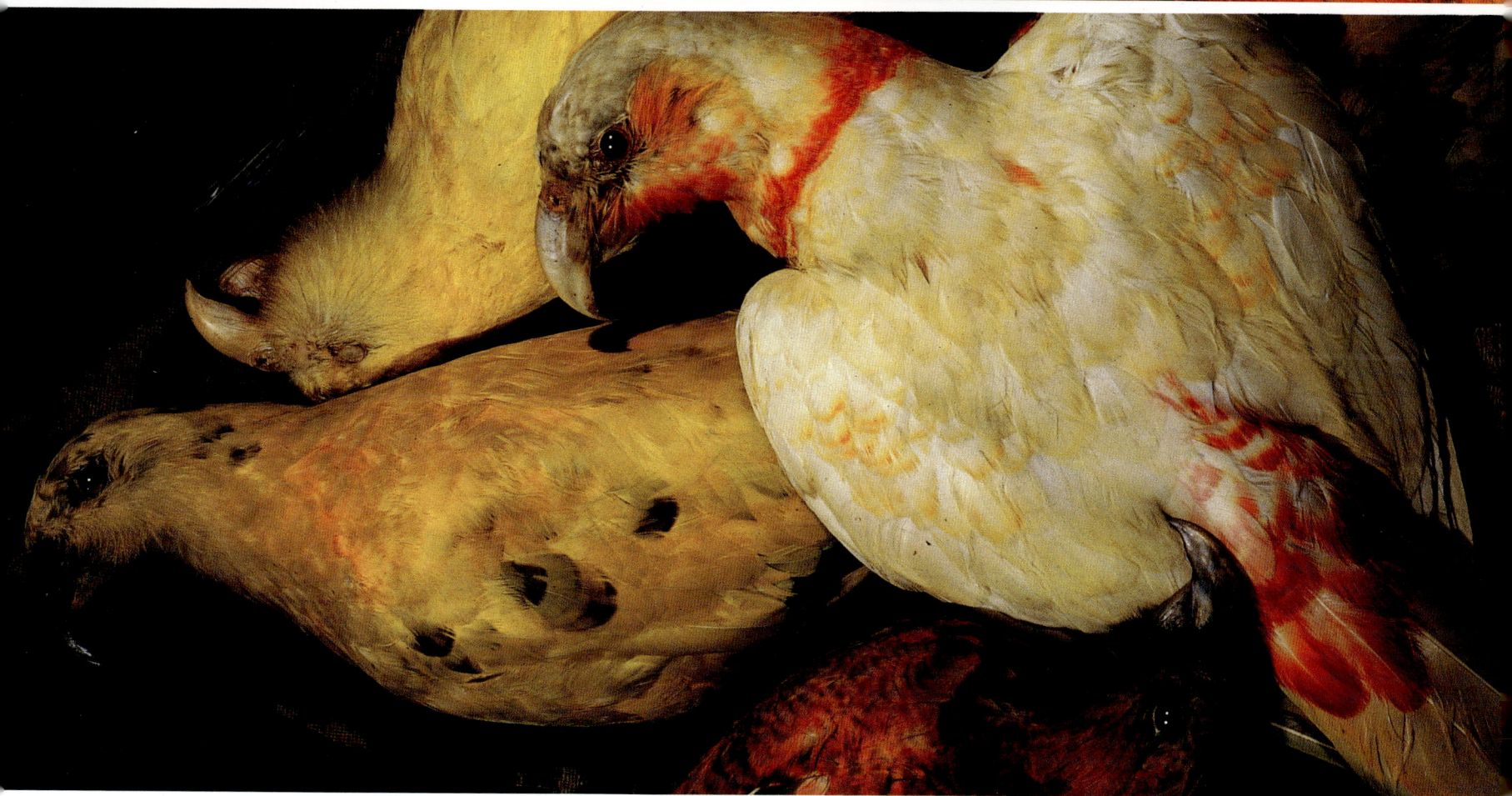

Common and widespread components of the now vanished dryland mosaic forest were nikau palms and native pigeons (*right*), moreporks and cabbage trees (*above right*), and insects such as the copper butterfly (*above*). Unlike the remains of birds and reptiles, insect remains are seldom preserved. Other less common species may have simply disappeared without our ever knowing of their existence.

Some spectacular members of the dryland mosaic forest flora are now among our rarest plants. These three different species of flowering tree broom (*above* and *left*) are extremely rare and widely scattered in remnant populations extending from Marlborough to South Canterbury. Usually to be found perched out of harm's way on bluffs (*far left*), the surviving plants are mere shadows of the large trees that once grew to great age and size in gentler country. The tree brooms have become the innocent victims of agricultural herbicides, as well as noxious browsing animals such as possums and goats.

Many members of the dryland mosaic forest fauna are now rare and scattered. Top predators such as the tuatara (*top left*) and its common prey Hamilton's frog (*left*) are to be found only in tiny remnant populations in places such as remote Stephens Island just outside the Marlborough Sounds. Other inhabitants such as the cabbage tree moth (*above*) are still relatively common although easily overlooked even in our own back yards.

A COUPLE OF SONG AND DANCE GUYS

CHAPTER FOUR

IT'S CABARET EVERY SUMMER NIGHT ON LITTLE BARRIER ISLAND. The forest on the steep volcanic flanks is reasonably quiet by day, but come nightfall it's as if the tall kauri columns themselves are making music. The strident riffs, protracted harmonies, lyric solos and pulsating rhythm all come from the animals that live on this island of survival.

When viewed from the coast north of Auckland a cloud cap often sits over the peaks of distant Little Barrier. The island's Maori name is Hauturu, the meeting place of the wind. The winds have blown many changes to this island during its short human history. Most recently the wild cat population was eliminated by a military-style poisoning campaign. Since their introduction a century earlier cats had wreaked havoc among the forest birds. In the colonies of burrowing sea birds 90 per cent of chicks were slaughtered by cats each season. The cats were removed in the 1970s.

With the cats gone the birds recovered. The island then became a lifeboat for rare native species that were facing uncertain futures elsewhere. Kokako, kakapo, saddleback and stitchbird now all thrive in its two and a half thousand hectares of kauri and mixed forest. One of these recent arrivals is a star performer in the summer cabaret of the night. Kakapo, the flightless parrot, is a passionate dancer. It joins an unlikely singer, a tiny bat that is smaller than a mouse.

All of New Zealand would once have pulsed with evening cabaret every bit as vibrant as that to be heard on Little Barrier Island. Some of the performers would have been daytime birds that couldn't sleep. Kaka are well-known insomniacs out on the island. Their honeyed calls rise in sweet purity only to fall in a cacophony of gurgles, squeaks and splutters. Little blue penguins and Cook's and black petrels also seem to need little sleep and add their cooing and cackling vocals to the sounds of the night. Other creatures, such as the kakapo and short-tailed bat, only come out at night. This is their time to feed, to fight and to go courting.

AND TONIGHT, FROM THE LEK, WE PRESENT... The show starts early most summer nights except when the weather is bad. Tonight the sun has barely set behind the hazy hills of distant Northland

A parrot like no other, New Zealand's flightless kakapo is the heaviest parrot in the world. It is also nocturnal and secretive, with an amazing song and dance routine.

when several small dark shapes explode from a hole in the trunk of an ancient puriri tree. Male short-tailed bats race swiftly and unerringly among the trees, following an invisible aerial highway along the valley into darkness. Each bat senses the obstacles in its path using echolocation. It emits a constant high-frequency sound beam which bounces back warning clicks to its sensitive ears when approaching a branch or tree trunk. The males head for prominent trees along this fly-way and quickly take up station in well-known holes in the trunks.

As the last of evening's light disappears from the valley, each of the male bats which has managed to secure a hole begins to sing. Its squeaky melody is a song of invitation to the female bats that have begun to fly along the same route to the feeding trees. Positioned at strategic intervals along the flight path, the males envelop the females in an avenue of love song.

The cabaret is the central act of the short-tailed bat's highly unusual form of courtship. The tree in which the male performs its enchanting evensong is called a lek (from Scandinavian *leka*, to play). The use by males of a display arena is a behavioural characteristic of a small group of mammals, fish, birds and insects, and is a specialised sexual strategy that can only be employed in a safe and benevolent environment. Kakapo is another lek species, the male having an arena or playground from where it solicits passing females first with song and then with dance.

Both male and female kakapo begin preparing for breeding many months before the long nights of summer. These large, flightless parrots are gourmets of the forest. They travel great distances each night to a single shrub or tree where fruit or foliage is at its best. Hauling their large bodies up into the branches they then feed luxuriously on the chosen food. Even though breeding may be more than a year away, the trigger for kakapo to begin their preparation for that event may be just one forest food. What factor or plant hormone contained in which fruit, seed or leaf causes this invisible change remains a mystery, but like a magic potion it will slowly prepare both male and female for the season

A kakapo chick, 26 days old and weighing 723 grams, photographed on Little Barrier Island after breeding took place in March 1991.

ahead. He must have the stamina required for months of night-time singing to attract a female for whom he will then dance. She then must have the strength and resources to lay, to incubate and to raise the offspring of their union on her own.

In spring male kakapo spend weeks preparing their arenas on the lek, along the ridge tops leading up to the island summit. Using beak and feet they move leaves and soil to shape circular depressions or "bowls" in the earth. The male at the top of each ridge is the dominant bird. One of these has completed his bowl. He now clears tracks in towards it by pulling seedlings and cutting surface roots with his bill. One of these neatly prepared paths will later lead a female, attracted by his song, to the bowl, where he will dance for her before they mate.

THE NIGHT HAS A THOUSAND EARS   The bats, down in the valley, have been singing lustily for a full half hour before the first kakapo comes to his bowl on the ridge. He is alert to every night sound. Just below the ridge, Cook's petrels crash-land close to their burrows. He stops to listen. A male kiwi shrieks over on the next ridge. Again he listens intently. Finally satisfied that all is in order, he settles into his bowl as if on a nest and begins to inflate air sacs in his chest.

As he inhales, the male makes a hissing sound rather like a bicycle pump, while his moss-coloured plumage begins to expand. Soon his whole body has become rounded in shape, and after a minute he has blown himself up to resemble a large feathered football with a small head on top. This is the bizarre prelude to his performance, which he now begins.

To say the male kakapo sings is rather stretching the definition of that word. He makes two sounds. One is a series of metallic-sounding rasps, called chinging. The other is a low, booming chant that sounds like someone blowing across the top of an empty bottle, delivered in bursts of perhaps 30 seconds' duration. After each set he pauses to listen. The night is alive with sound as the cabaret gets into full swing. The kakapo is alert to it all. He also listens for the distant shriek of recognition made

84

A male short-tailed bat feeds on the parasitic flower of *Dactylanthus taylorii* on Little Barrier Island. It is only recently that New Zealand's sole native mammal has been discovered to be an important pollinator of this extraordinary subterranean plant.

only by a kakapo female. Throughout the night he repeats his pattern of booming chant followed by silence, over and over.

He seems to have no control over the sound he makes. Each "boom" rises up like a bout of hiccups and rocks his body with effort. It seems to travel in both air and earth at the same time, over great distance, giving the forest a deep rhythm that accompanies the other calls and cries from all over the island.

From the valley can be heard a distinctive sound, a chorus of high-pitched "cheeps". These are the calls of the bats, which have been performing for four hours without a break. One tiny tenor is holed up high in a large, stately cylinder of kauri. So far he has sung inside his hole, then crooned with his head at the entrance. To make his stage more alluring he now urinates outside on the trunk and rubs the strong scent around the entrance. He is tired but he resumes his love song.

In the trees nearby, other ears hear that his song is beginning to fade. Several male bats wait for him to falter, their cue to make a bid to take over his stage, his hole. One swoops in anticipation, only to be brought to the ground in a dogfighting tumble. The singer quickly recaptures his place in the avenue. He continues his song, tired but not beaten. A short time later another dark shape swoops into the hole. This time there is no altercation — only silence. Within the chamber the male mates with a female he may never see again. His part in the procreative process is then over. He may mate with others, but male short-tailed bats, like all lek males, play no further part in caring for and raising offspring.

Short-tailed bats are the only mammals to have survived in New Zealand through the long dynasty of birds. Though fast fliers they spend considerable time on the forest floor. They stalk their insect prey on oversized legs, which give them the appearance of mice on stilts. They are also pollinators of a variety of related flowers including *Astelia*, nikau and kiekie. Bats have recently been discovered to be the principal pollinators of the flowering root parasite *Dactylanthus*, to which they are attracted by its strong, musky aroma.

THE LAST DANCE   The kakapo, a heavyweight among parrots, is quite incapable of flying. Other parrots can quickly become airborne and pursue a potential mate above the glittering foliage and away over hills and valleys to consummate their union. During the breeding season male kakapo, the only flightless lek birds in the world, return to their arenas every night of summer.

The male at the top of the ridge has been visited by two females in two months of nightly booming. He has done better than others. His basso profundo and dominant position seem to have swung things in his favour. Tonight he is again lucky.

At first he only hears the female's call. This is sufficient incentive to redouble his booming effort. Soon his eyes flash with excitement as she approaches up his carefully gardened path.

The female is uncertain, distracted. She looks round and pecks at leaves. To prove his worthiness in her eyes he stops booming, spreads his wings wide and begins a slow dance around her. He rocks gently from side to side, opening and closing each flightless wing alternately like a mime artist locked in his routine. It is utterly beguiling. The female's manner changes; she makes fewer nervous movements as the dance continues.

Lek birds of the day include the bowerbirds of Australia and New Guinea, the males of which build elaborate bowers-like display grounds in the breeding season to attract females, and various species

An empty stage (*far left*). By day, a male kakapo's bowl, with a carefully clipped and maintained track passing before it, lies silent after the night's activity on a Stewart Island ridge. After dark (*left and above*), the occupant returns to boom his lovelorn cries in his quest for a mate. The grainy, ghost-like images from a zeniscope reveal this extraordinary, secret, night-time ritual.

of grouse that boom and show off their colours and crests. The kakapo is the only nocturnal lek bird in the world. To attract a female the male uses his voice and his hypnotising dance. With wings forward like a cape, he shuffles on slow feet as if answering the rhythm of the night. It is a simple thing, this dance, yet effective. The female finally presents to mate, a union which takes place like everything to do with kakapo — slowly.

The eccentric behaviour of the singing bat and the song and dance parrot is in stark contrast to a world in which most mammals and birds form pair bonds in order to share the duties of raising young. It would seem that sharing the work of family life makes survival easier, but there is also good sense in males investing all their time in competing with other males at the lek. To the females the male show-offs are like objects on a supermarket shelf, from among which they select the biggest or the best of the species.

This type of "shopping around" sexual selection does build a stronger society, but it can only take place when conditions are highly favourable. Lek behaviour requires an environment in which there is an abundance of food, so the female can raise the young on her own, and which is free of the kinds of predators that would strike down the male as he performs his bizarre cabaret of the night. Such behaviour in modern New Zealand is risky to say the least.

A mottled green male kakapo dances to an imagined mate deep in the forests of Fiordland. With the coming of dawn the dancing parrot once again melts into the forest (*left*), his carefully camouflaged body concealing it from the view of even the closest passer-by.

From a crevice in a totara tree, a male short-tailed bat sings for a mate. The entrance to his hole is heavily stained with urine and musky grease, which also serve as attractants. He will sing at the entrance to the hole until he is exhausted, when another male will make an attempt to oust him and try his luck. Should a female arrive she will be invited inside the hole, where the couple will mate in privacy.

Burrowing bat or flying mole? With unusually robust hind legs, and front wings that fold away into grooves in its forelimbs, the short-tailed bat is able to spend much of its life scrambling on or under the ground in search of flightless insects to eat. It has a voracious appetite, hunting large prey such as burrowing huhu grubs (*above*), weta in petrel burrows (*below left*) and native cockroaches living in the forest litter (*below right*).

Right: The short-tailed bat has tiny eyes, sharp teeth and a pig-like snout for nosing out prey. Its velvety "moleskin" coat sheds dirt as easily as the coat of any real mole as it delves and forages.

GALLERY OF THE ANCIENTS

CHAPTER FIVE

THE TITLE OF THIS CHAPTER READS LIKE the name of a hall in a museum, and in a way it is. The lineage of amphibians and reptiles found in New Zealand spans 200 million years, more than half the entire period of life on earth. Some exhibits have endured not just the violent upheavals that have been part of the adolescence of these islands, but have survived periods of worldwide mass extinctions, including one that saw the end of the last dynasty of reptiles, the fall of the dinosaurs. Here in New Zealand, this isolated archipelago in the southwest Pacific Ocean, a few priceless relics from the past are still to be found living.

THE COOL REPTILE AND THE PONDLESS FROG   On Stephens Island at the entrance to Cook Strait, a male tuatara has stood like a stone statue for 40 minutes. Its body temperature is 10 degrees Celsius, the same as the windy hillside on which he waits.

Nearby, in a burrow, a female tuatara crunches the skull of a fairy prion chick. She has shared this burrow, one of thousands on the island, with the prion pair right through their courtship, egg laying and incubation and the first three weeks of their chick's life. The adult birds have even climbed all over her when returning to their burrow from feeding at sea. On this night, however, she has just killed their chick. She eats only the skull and brain. Perhaps she needs extra protein at this time to promote the development of the eggs inside her — or maybe she is just hungry.

Soon after dusk she emerges from the burrow, close to the larger, solitary male. The scales on his back and head rise, giving him the appearance of a small dragon. They also give him his Maori name, tuatara — line of spears.

Half of all tuatara now live on Stephens Island. Each night, out on the forest floor and the shrubby slopes, more than 30,000 of them are active — although, as regards tuatara, the term "active" is perhaps relative only. Any movement is followed by long periods of inactivity. The one deed that does involve prolonged action, on the part of the male at least, is sex.

Strange bedfellows: a fairy prion shares its nesting chamber with a female tuatara. While the partnership appears amicable, tuatara will eat prion eggs, chicks and even adults from time to time.

The aroused male has been courting the female for at least 40 minutes. His overtures have consisted of circling her using a sort of reptilian goose step known as the *stolzergang*. While performing this strut, he is upright with his throat expanded. Up until now, each time he has approached her, she has attempted to retreat and he has lunged at her and bitten her neck. This time she doesn't retreat and he is no longer aggressive.

The male carefully mounts the female, who slowly moves forward but does not dislodge him. He then clasps her with one rear leg and slips his tail beneath hers. Lacking any sort of penile organ, he places his cloaca beside hers and sperm is placed between their bodies to be taken up by the female.

The whole process has taken perhaps an hour. This was the fast part. The rest of the breeding cycle is very slow. A summer mating may not result in egg laying until the following spring. At this time, a female digs a burrow in a nursery area, usually in a north-facing bank of earth where underground temperatures remain a few degrees Celsius warmer than in the soil of the shaded forest floor.

Having laid 10 or more eggs, the female half refills the hole and waits beside it. For the next few nights she stands guard to prevent other egg laying females from re-excavating her burrow and disturbing her eggs. She then closes the burrow completely and leaves her clutch to slowly develop.

Depending on soil temperature, it may take a year or more for the eggs to hatch (making tuatara incubation the longest of any reptile). The babies then emerge into a dangerous world. The pale brown bodies that erupt from the earth in a jumble are everything that adult tuatara are not. They are agile creatures that dart after insect prey and then fight each other for ownership of a tasty meal. They may not be fast enough, however, to avoid the lightning-fast lunge of bigger jaws. A newly hatched tuatara lies limply in the mouth of an adult of its own kind. Tuatara, like many of their reptile relations among the lizards, snakes and crocodiles, are experts in the art of "wait and pounce" hunting.

From among the rocks near the top of Stephens Island, a number of tiny frogs emerge at night to feed. The ancestry of these modest creatures stretches back further than the tuatara's. The prospect of an ancient eating another animal of even greater antiquity seems highly unfortunate, yet tuatara will eat Hamilton's frogs quite oblivious of the fact that the age of the *Amphibia* preceded the age of reptiles and that these frogs, like tuatara, belong to the select group of founding families of New Zealand animals.

Frogs and water usually go together, yet there are no ponds, streams or puddles close to the colony of Hamilton's frogs, found near the summit of the island. These frogs are one of four species of the tiny leiopelmatid frogs, found only in New Zealand. They have webless feet and live among the rocks in a high-and-dry fashion.

Unlike most frogs, leiopelmatids do not have free-swimming tadpoles. Instead, the tadpoles meta-morphose inside gelatinous capsules, their own personal ponds. They emerge after a month as small frogs and climb on their father's back, where they remain until their remnant tails are lost and they are able to pursue independent lives. Curiously, these frogs are also croakless and earless.

The homes of Hamilton's frogs are not as dry as first appears. Stephens Island is frequently capped with cloud, and the rocks in which the frogs find shelter are riddled with deep, damp chambers. Here is sufficient moisture for the frogs' respiratory needs and to maintain the development of their eggs.

It appears that both tuatara and frogs were once extremely plentiful on forest floors in many parts of New Zealand, particularly in the now vanished dryland mosaic forest of the eastern South Island. While tuatara have been driven from the mainland by the depredation of rats, the frogs, though heavily decimated, have been more resilient and may exist in more locations than we tend to assume.

In the North Island, the closely related but smaller Archey's frog is to be found on the Coromandel Peninsula. By day, this frog conceals itself beneath rocks up on ridges or down in stream beds. Under torchlight, at night, pairs of tiny red eyes reflect back from rocks and tree trunks. Archey's frogs have managed to survive here, close to tracks and in the presence of rats and other predators.

The search has now begun for Hamilton's frogs on the hilltops of the Marlborough Sounds. Will they, too, prove to be mainland survivors like Archey's frogs, or do they only hold out where many from the Gallery of the Ancients find sole sanctuary — on offshore islands?

RICHES OF THE POOR KNIGHTS   On one of his voyages, navigator and explorer Captain James Cook sailed close to a group of islands east of Northland and near the edge of the continental shelf. Having mapped the three large and several small islands, he named them the Poor Knights after a well-known English pudding! Had Cook gone ashore he may have been moved to give the islands a more ro-mantic, or in some respect more befitting, title. However, as his crew may also have accidentally taken stowaway rats ashore, we forgive him his omission and the peculiar name he bestowed on these fabu-lous islands.

Normally a night stalker of insect prey and "sipper" of nectar, a Pacific gecko emerges in bright daylight to scavenge regurgitated fish dropped by a gannet chick.

Above the sheer cliffs, in summer, the forest canopy is blood red with pohutukawa flowers. Korimako (bellbirds) flit noisily from one nectar-filled floral cup to the next. Their full-throated calls give the impression that this is a forest of many birds. Certainly there are plenty of bellbirds. Hosts of sea birds use the islands too, but only as a summer breeding platform. That task completed they depart, leaving the forests to the bellbirds, kakariki (parakeets) and two small species of rail. The Poor Knights' is a very simple ecosystem in which the work of the birds and the bees is just as likely to be performed by reptiles.

In the late afternoon the shadow of a homecoming gannet traces the shoreline, causing a gleaming snake-like shape to slither into a rock pool. This Suter's skink dog-paddles to the bottom of the pool and waits until it decides that danger is past. It is the only one of nearly 60 species of lizard in New Zealand that swims proficiently.

Danger past, the skink returns to the surface to begin its work of egg laying in light gravel close to the pool, thereby revealing another of its unique features: it is the only New Zealand lizard to lay eggs. All other species hold eggs in the oviduct or egg-carrying tube until they hatch, then give birth to live young.

Fifty-nine species from the two great families of lizards, the *Scincidae* (skinks) and the *Gekkonidae* (geckos), are represented in New Zealand. In other parts of the world live birth is unusual but not unknown among the shiny ground-dwelling lizards known as skinks. Among the scaly, bulgy-eyed geckos of the world, however, live birth is unknown, except among the 29 species found on the islands of New Zealand and by one close relative in New Caledonia. The temperate land of New Zealand is cool by lizard standards. By retaining and carrying her eggs, a lizard mother may keep them warmer for longer, thereby helping her offspring to develop faster than in eggs laid in the earth. (The New Caledonian species bears live young, but in warmer conditions has been known to lay eggs.)

The gannet, having landed among the drawn daggers of its neighbours' bills on Sugerloaf Rock Stack, has fed its chick until it is full to overflowing. Now the youngster vomits up the excess fish slurry. Immediately, lizards appear from all directions to devour the discarded fish. Then the gulls arrive and drive them back to the protection of the rocks. Every rock seems to have a moving shadow of Pacific geckos. Out on this barren outcrop these normally nocturnal fruit and insect eaters have become highly successful daytime scavengers.

As night falls Pacific geckos that keep more regular hours come out on Aorangi Island, one of the larger of the Poor Knights group. They join Duvaucel's gecko, New Zealand's largest surviving gecko, up in the branches of the pohutukawa trees. Both species are drawn to the nectar cups of the brush-like flowers that have been slowly refilling since the bellbirds ceased feeding and went to their evening roosts. Within a short time the canopy is crawling with small, scaly bodies that move from flower to flower licking up the rich, honeyed liquid.

As they drink, the geckos' chins are tickled by the pollen-laden pohutukawa stamens. Tiny projections on the scales of their necks trap small quantities of pollen. The geckos then transport the pollen to the next flower or the neighbouring tree. The work of these pollinators of the night is not confined to pohutukawa. The geckos of the Poor Knights also pollinate the rock lily *Xeronema callistemon* and flax. Naturally, they have not lost their taste for fruit.

On summer nights the excesses of the gecko banquet up in the trees are more than matched by the feastings below on the forest floor. The islands resound to the cackles and coos of insomniac sea birds of many species. Among the sea bird burrows a tuatara lunges at a skink that has just hunted a spider. The leaf litter crackles with invertebrate predators and prey. There is food aplenty in this reptilian paradise, which is surely an Aotearoan wildlife treasure chest.

A TALE OF TWO SKINKS   In the late 1960s a colony of large, intensely patterned skinks was discovered at Pukerua Bay near Wellington, on a boulder bank just above the high tide mark. They were examined, described and duly assigned the name *Cyclodina whitakeri*, after herpetologist Tony Whitaker. Their genus name, *Cyclodina*, put these new discoveries alongside other members of the ancient Gondwanan group of nocturnal, tropical skinks found in the North Island. Small cyclodinids such as copper skinks and rata skinks live in urban Auckland, but most of the larger ones are restricted to offshore islands. It is ironic that 200-millimetre-long heavyweights such as *Cyclodina macgregori* and *Cyclodina alani* endure only on islands without rats, but the reason is simple — these skinks are so big that they cannot squeeze into crevices small enough to hide from their mammalian predators. Wherever they go, rats can follow, and in the North Island their journey has led them to extinction. So how did *Cyclodina whitakeri* (Whitaker's skink) survive all that time on the beach at Pukerua Bay? The answer is that it is protected by the deep and confusing jumble of rocks of its boulder-bank home.

A few years after the discovery near Wellington, another colony of Whitaker's skinks was found on an island in the Mercury group east of Coromandel Peninsula. That the two colonies of identical skinks were 500 kilometres apart raised a simple question. How? The only logical explanation is that Whitaker's skinks, which are a little smaller than heavyweight, were once to be found in many places between (and probably beyond) these two locations. The discoveries of Whitaker's skinks remind us of the probability that many of New Zealand's remaining wild treasures — birds and invertebrates as well as reptiles — once commanded much greater ranges of territory than they presently occupy. This notion is graphically demonstrated by two members of the second skink family, the southerners or leiolopismids.

Whitaker's skink has a strangely distinct distribution. A tiny population endures at Pukerua Bay near Wellington. The only other places in which this skink is now found are two tiny islands off the northern coast, perhaps indicating that it once had a more continuous distribution throughout the North Island.

The jutting tors, or stacks, of schist rock in the harsh Central Otago landscape give the appearance of Wild West country. These rocks have become the refuges (or stockades) of two lizards whose continued survival is becoming increasingly precarious. Being diurnal, or daytime, creatures, they are put under siege by wild cats and birds. Tussock burning and pasture sowing have isolated them, too, such that an ocean of green grass now laps around their islands of rock. Some of these islands have been protected by conservation workers and a few lizard-loving farmers, but this might not be enough. Unlike the big, northern cyclodinids that have predator-free offshore islands for refuge, the two Otago leiolopismid skinks have only their rocky, feline-haunted Central Otago islands to cling to.

SEARCHING HIGH AND LOW   A manuka bush in a field on Otago Peninsula is home to a gecko that is an expert in disguise. The first, telltale sign of its presence is the recently moulted skin that hangs over a branch, rather like a pair of pale tights put out to dry on a clothesline. On coming closer, a sharp "chek chek" sound is heard, but it is only with the greatest difficulty that the maker of the sound is finally spotted. The markings on *Naultinus gemmeus* (the jewelled gecko) blend superbly with the bush it lives on. As it moves, the gecko grasps a branch with exceedingly long fingers and makes use of its tail as a prehensile fifth limb.

The jewelled gecko is the most stunningly attractive member of the long-fingered, elegantly marked, daytime tree climbers called *Naultinus*, found throughout New Zealand. Most have more green and less patterning than the jewelled gecko, but all share in having a vividly coloured mouth that loves to be filled with nectar, fruit and the occasional insect.

It was quite by chance that in 1969 the southernmost gecko in the world was discovered near the bottom of Stewart Island. Low cloud, low temperatures and a landscape of stunted vegetation and granite outcrops would seem less than an ideal habitat, but in this environment was found a wonderfully patterned green gecko that came to be known as the harlequin gecko. First impressions were that this was another green tree gecko, but it was not.

The harlequin gecko turned out to belong to the second great group of New Zealand geckos, called *Hoplodactylus*. Unlike the sun-loving green tree geckos, *Hoplodactylus* geckos are brown, ground

An artist's model of the now extinct Delcourt's gecko, at one time the largest lizard in the world. Depicted here stalking a giant weta, this truly spectacular member of the New Zealand reptile fauna could also have fed on other giant invertebrates.

dwelling and nocturnal. *Hoplodactylus rakiurae*, the harlequin gecko, is a nonconformist. It has abandoned the drab, brown livery of other *Hoplodactylus* geckos and adopted a wonderfully patterned green colour for a life among the stunted trees of Stewart Island.

In 1970 another nonconforming *Hoplodactylus* gecko was discovered, this time high in the Seaward Kaikoura mountains. The colour of the black-eyed gecko, *Hoplodactylus kahutarae*, is conformist, but uncharacteristically it possesses long, curving fingers like those of a green tree gecko. These are the fingers of an accomplished rock climber. Black-eyed geckos chase alpine insects across rock bluffs and up and down cliffs with consummate ease. They live well above the winter snow line, and when snow comes they can hibernate deep within rock crevices for months at a time. These little mountain-climbing geckos have laid down a challenge. If they can survive the extreme conditions of the Seaward Kaikoura, where will the next lizard discovery take place?

A discovery of yet another *Hoplodactylus* gecko took place in 1990 against the background of the New Zealand sesquicentennial celebrations. A few years earlier, a single, very large gecko, almost twice the size of any known species, came to light in a collection at the Natural History Museum in Marseille, France. The animal had been dead for more than a century but it was identified as a *Hoplodactylus* gecko. This placed it among eight similar, but much smaller, species of gecko found only in New Zealand with the exception of a single species from New Caledonia. When this monster gecko arrived here in 1990 as a centre-piece for a "Forgotten Fauna" display, interest and speculation became intense. Could it be the legendary kawekaweau from the North Island? Was this gecko the same as that known from a few bones in the South Island? A research team went to work x-raying and sampling whatever they could, from DNA to parasites. The results remain tantalisingly ambiguous.

The stuffed specimen of *Hoplodactylus delcourti* was later returned to France and all we are left with is possibilities. Was this creature a giant tree-dwelling gecko that lived in northern (or southern) forests of New Zealand? Researchers must now get busy. Not only are they combing remote and inaccessible parts of the country for more new, eccentric species of live *Hoplodactylus* gecko, but they are also searching caves and dunes for skeletal remains of an old, and probably extinct, eccentric, which if found will take pride of place in New Zealand's extraordinary Gallery of the Ancients.

Just on sunset an adult tuatara emerges from its burrow on Stephens Island, close to the Marlborough Sounds. Although tuatara survive on nearly 30 of New Zealand's offshore islands, fully half the remaining population lives on this one island.

After a year slowly developing inside the egg, a young tuatara emerges. It will lead a dangerous life on the forest floor, being at risk from a number of predators, including adult tuatara.

New Zealand's largest and most spectacular skinks are seldom seen today. They include the robust skink (*above left*), a large, square, chunky, nocturnal creature now found only on two northern offshore islands. The Three Kings Island skink (*top left*) is seen here consuming kawakawa fruit on the forest floor. The chevron skink (*top right*) is now confined to Little and Great Barrier Islands. Such large skinks are endangered because of the depredation of rats, which can follow them into their crevice hiding places and attack them. Our smaller skinks are more effective at concealing and survive on the mainland today in the presence of rats. Some, such as the common southern skink (*above right*), are beautifully camouflaged.

A Suter's skink, New Zealand's only egg-laying skink, swims in a rock pool after dark in the Poor Knights Islands. This shore-dweller is a remarkably strong swimmer; its ancestors may in fact have "rafted" here from Australia.

The jewelled gecko (*above*) and the rough-skinned gecko (*right*) from Marlborough are experts at camouflage. When removed from their environment they are revealed as intricately and boldly patterned, but among foliage they disappear completely as they lie in wait for insects.

Above: Two forest geckos share their winter home in a hollow tree with a colony of tree weta.
Right: The small and recently discovered harlequin gecko from Stewart Island has a beautifully patterned body that rivals the "green" geckos for colour and design.

Right: A green gecko displays its bright blue mouth as it "barks" at camera. Blue berries are an unusual feature of some New Zealand plants; their colour may once have attracted feeding geckos.
Centre right: An albino common gecko lacks any pigment in its skin at all.
Far right: A female forest gecko accompanies her twin offspring on a moss-covered branch. All our geckos bear live young (invariably twins), whereas geckos overseas lay eggs.

Above: Beautifully camouflaged, a Hochstetter's frog sits on a wet rock waiting for its prey to pass at night.
Top right: A male Archey's frog broods a clutch of eggs.
Right: Soon after hatching, the tiny tailed froglets climb onto the male's hind legs and up onto his back. Here they spend their final weeks of development.

FLIGHTLESS GIANTS

CHAPTER SIX

"COULD YOU THROW ANOTHER LOG ON THE FIRE?"   It is an innocent request such as this that can change attitudes for life.

The hand that casually reaches out to pick up the manuka log looms towards an accidental hitchhiker. The male tree weta has remained with the log for 6 months since its shrinking forest was cut down. The insect's hind legs are pulled forward over its head in warning. The hand comes closer. The weta now employs its last line of defence — it bites.

What follows is pandemonium. There is a lot of yelling. The hapless insect is then squashed, incinerated and, along with all its kin, cursed for ever. And so a hatred of weta is born into another family mythology.

"Remember when Mum got bitten by that huge weta. It was gross."

"I hate them too. I put my gumboots on once and there was one inside — I screamed."

Such mythology arises as part of creepy-crawly mystique. In New Zealand there are no snakes or scorpions and only one poisonous spider to inspire our fears, so we invent our horrible creepy-crawlies by misrepresenting creatures we do have. The most likely candidates for such notoriety are weta. They are big and brown and possess a frightening array of long legs and antennae with which they score high on a fearsome looks scale, but most score virtually zero on a fearsome behaviour scale.

Weta do not deserve an evil reputation. They belong to a benign group of insects called *Orthopterans* (meaning straight wing), and are grasshoppers that have become flightless. This characteristic is by no means unusual in New Zealand, a place which does rather specialise in flightlessness. There are flightless weevils, beetles and stick insects, and of course all those flightless birds.

Many flightless insects have become giants in New Zealand, and the most spectacular examples are to be found among weta, which are without rivals in diversity of shape and function. Weta can be divided into four main groups: cave weta, ground weta, giant weta and tree weta.

Now is probably as good a time as any to ask which tree weta it was on the log that caused the

The source of all fierce weta stories: a male West Coast tree weta, or taipo, glares from his hole in a rotten log. These, the most aggressive of our tree weta, have a nasty bite when disturbed.

family panic. The answer depends rather on where the log came from. Wood piles from the Far North to Levin conceal Auckland tree weta. Wellington tree weta then take over and are found in wood piles on both sides of Cook Strait and down the West Coast as far as Haast. On the eastern side of the South Island there are Canterbury and Otago tree weta, although the Otago tree weta, in order to escape rats, resides exclusively under rocks in the mountains. There are one or two other localised tree weta but one in particular deserves a mention. The West Coast has a second, larger tree weta called the taipo (or devil). This is the most aggressive tree weta of all. Its bite would make a logger run, and it is highly likely that much of the weta's evil reputation stems from taipo stories over on the Coast.

GENTLE GIANTS   There are a number of claimants to the title of New Zealand's Elder States-species. Both the ancient tuatara and the native frogs put forward a strong case for the honour, but our giant weta should not be overlooked. Their principle claim is based on findings of fossil insects in Queensland. These stony sentinels, which appear to be surprisingly similar to our giant weta, lived and flourished 180 million years ago.

Life for a giant weta begins in the earth as a 7-millimetre-long egg, which splits open in the spring to reveal the young weta nymph. The grasshopper-green youngster climbs into the welcoming branches of a nearby shrub, where it soon changes colour to brown and settles down to spend the next two years eating, growing and shedding its rigid exoskeleton approximately 10 times. This is an unusually long juvenile period for an insect, and having taken such a leisurely time to reach adulthood, giant weta have only six months more to live. They spend the greater proportion of this time on the ground foraging, like insect cows, for plant food. They are lumbering, peaceable creatures, whose only defence is to raise their spiny back legs above their heads.

Their other task during adulthood is to breed. A female will lay 200–300 eggs in regular batches during her remaining months. Each night she will be attended by males, attracted by her strong scent.

111

Having completed their respective procreative assignments, both male and female weta will die, and from her eggs will arise the new generation.

INSECT MICE   Mana Island is a squat pancake of land that lies off the southwest corner of the North Island. It is frequently overlooked in favour of the impressive profile of Kapiti Island further up the coast, yet Mana, in its unassuming way, has proved to be the setting for a real wildlife success story.

Mana Island has been many things — home for Maori hapu and farmers, a quarantine station and now a wildlife reserve. During some of its previous lives, Mana Island was populated by mice. The removal of farm animals in the late 1980s caused pasture to go to seed, and mice numbers exploded into a plague of millions. What followed was a remarkable effort to recover the island. A plan was devised to rid the entire 217 hectare Mana Island of mice in a double-hit poisoning campaign in 1989. Miraculously it worked. Mice were completely eradicated, and within two years the island had been transformed. This was graphically evident when walking with a torch at night. What could not be seen was heard. A sickening crunch underfoot was a sign that yet another giant weta had been squashed. It could not be helped. The plague of mice had become a plague of weta — and during a night-time stroll it was now possible to meet the clan.

Once the eye keens to the task, it is quite easy to find them. On the ground beside the track, the torch picks out the unmistakable dimpled outline of a huge, docile, female Cook Strait giant weta. She is harmless, being capable of neither jumping, biting nor stinging. Her main preoccupation, judging by her bulging abdomen, is to find a place to push her ovipositor into loose earth and lay tonight's clutch of eggs. She weighs close to 30 grams, the weight of two of the mice she and her kind have replaced in both numbers and function. Weta, like mice, emerge from daytime shelters and forage on greenery and seeds after dark. Also like mice they are polygamous, and even their droppings are mouse-like.

The savagery of weta increases in inverse proportion to size. The giants are gentle vegetarians, whereas the few Wellington tree weta that can now be seen in the lank grass will eat a mixed diet and are capable of biting. The males have strong jaws and very broad, slabby faces for their moderate-sized bodies. Any attempt to pick one up is greeted by the twin defences of spiny back legs raised and then jaws open in readiness to nip. Opportunity denied, the torch finally alights on a few very small weta out and about on the grass. They could be young nymphs of tree or giant weta, but closer inspection reveals them to be ground weta. They are just 20 millimetres long, dull in colour and unspectacular in aspect, but this modest appearance is deceptive. These are weta with an attitude. They are murderous carnivores that hunt worms, spiders and other ground invertebrates. Of all weta, these tiny, burrowing terrorists are the most to be feared — if you are a dweller in or under the leaf litter.

The weta plague on Mana Island is now over. The weta were not poisoned but have established populations in balance with the resources and the natural predators of the island. Mana Island has become a treasury for some of the most spectacular and unusual insects on Earth.

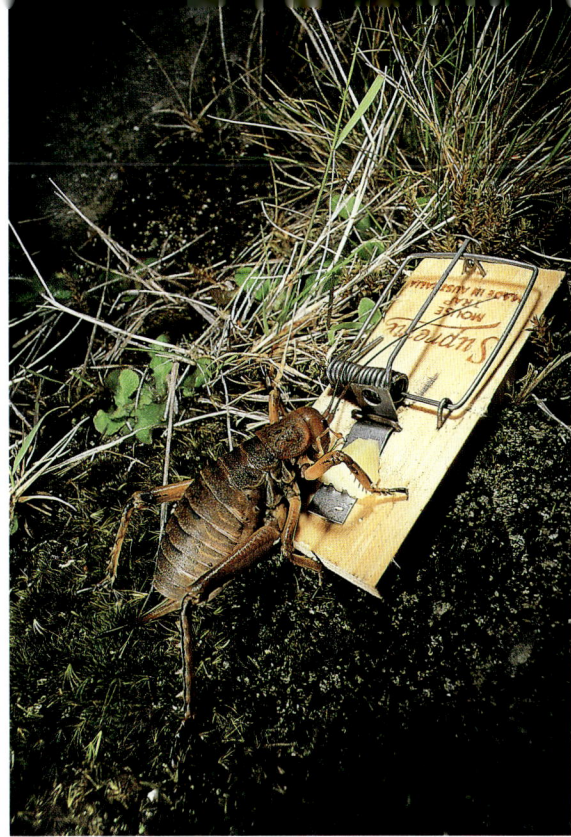

Often described by New Zealand entomologists as behaving more like invertebrate mice than insects, giant weta do like cheese and can be caught in mousetraps, as this large female demonstrates.

A GROUND WETA — WITH ANTLERS?   The largest and most bizarre ground weta have only recently been discovered. They are a massive four times the size of most others in their group. On the forest floor of a northern offshore island two male weta, each about 80 millimetres long, are locked in battle. On closer inspection they are seen to be jousting like stags. Both weta have a pair of long, curved tusks which they are using, like stags use their antlers, to flip their opponent. Finally one tusked weta gives up the ritualised joust and wanders off, uninjured but exhausted, across the leaf litter. The victor moves his tusks together backwards and forwards. The serrated edges produce a rasping sound, which may be a signal either to his competitor or a potential mate. Only males possess these long tusks, which do seem to get in the way when not being used in display or battle. As with all ground weta, their means of defence is located at the front end.

These spectacularly tusked ground weta remain creatures of mystery that we know only from a few individuals on one 10 hectare island in the outer Hauraki Gulf. Who would have imagined a few years ago that such bizarre creatures could ever exist? Weta continue to defy both imagination and expectation. New species of giant are still coming to light, and not only on offshore islands. Some have been found isolated on "ecological islands" on the New Zealand mainland.

ISLANDS WITHIN ISLANDS   Back in 1962 a school teacher from Mahoenui, in the King Country, alerted entomologists to a new giant weta that he had discovered on a nearby farm. This discovery was highly significant, as it meant that at least one species could not only endure loss of forest habitat but also live alongside mammalian predators. Over the next 20 years just a handful of individuals were found. They were obviously the last vestiges of a remnant species and hardly representatives of a new giant "wonderweta".

It is a brave man indeed who will handle a male West Coast tree weta, the taipo, but Paul Barret (*right*) from Wellington Zoo is just one of a number of individuals who are growing increasingly interested in these extraordinary insects. Weta scientist Dr Mary McIntyre (*far right*) searches for giant weta on Mana Island with the aid of a radio tracking device. Her subjects are large enough to carry their own radio transmitters and battery packs — something most insect scientists can only dream about.

Then a good-sized population was found nearby. They were living in, of all places, a large patch of gorse, a plant which is botanical Public Enemy Number One. More money is spent controlling gorse than any other weed in New Zealand, but at Mahoenui the 300 hectare forest of gorse has now been fenced off in a reserve as a sanctuary for the giant weta it protects. This arrangement is of benefit to both species. The spines of the gorse present a vast and impenetrable zone of defence for the weta against predators, for which service the gorse is saved. Though confined within this prickly fortress, the weta don't go hungry. Gorse is a nitrogen fixer and makes extremely good weta food.

Another new giant weta was found recently by trampers in the Paparoa Range. This is a giant that has learnt to burrow. Its "giant" status was confirmed by the male's habit of lying in his burrow using his extremely spiky back legs to protect the entrance. Giant mole weta, as its kind are now known, are vegetarians that live in deep burrows which are doglegged, probably as a defence against probing kiwi. True burrowing, however, is the preserve of ground weta. They always face the world and any danger head-on, not turning their backs on it like the newly discovered giant does.

Another giant weta discovery, made within the last five years, wasn't a burrower but a climber. It took a rock-climbing human to find the rock-climbing or Bluff weta close to Mt Somers in South Canterbury. This elegantly banded giant is protected from predators by a fortress of sheer rock in much the same way as the Mahoenui weta hides within its stronghold of gorse spines.

The recent discovery of these three giants has renewed scientific interest in weta. The tide of prejudice is turning away from our creepy-crawlies. There are now many, including children, who have become fascinated and enthusiastic supporters and collectors of these much maligned flightless grasshoppers that are like no other insects on Earth.

Giant weta credentials are impressive. They are the heaviest — and among the biggest — of the world's insects, which is no mean achievement in a multitude so vast it comprises 1.8 million species, or 80 per cent of life on Earth. If insects were to completely disappear, the remaining life on earth would probably end a short time later. Insects are the unsung heroes of planetary composting, soil making, shredding and recycling. Their vast hordes are ecologically vital and have evolved through time to perform a myriad tasks. However, within their innumerable ranks the venerable and ancient commanders of all insects must be the giant weta of New Zealand.

Above: A male giant weta follows a larger female on a feeding foray after dark. Pheromones in her droppings have enabled him to track and locate her at mating time.
Right: The heaviest insect in the world, her body distended by more than 300 eggs, a female giant weta quietly lays beneath the soil surface after dark.

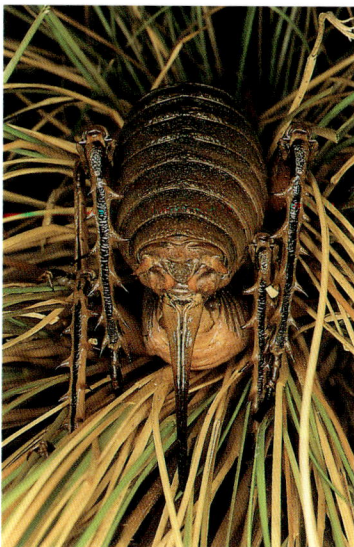

Above: Giant weta are gentle browsing giants which feed on a variety of plants, including moss. The small, finger-like palps around the female's jaws are really modified legs used for handling and manipulating food.
Left: The male almost concealed beneath the female, and their heads buried in a tussock clump, a pair of giant weta mate.

With strikingly coloured limbs of orange, black and white, a female Bluff weta from Mount Somers (*above*) raises her hind legs in typical giant weta threat, while a close-up of an adult male from a colony in the Seaward Kaikoura ranges (*right*) focuses on the more modest blue-grey and red-brown body colours that help camouflage the insect against the rocks. Giant weta are amongst the largest and heaviest insects in the world, yet, remarkably, new species are still being discovered each year.

Above: Like a creature from a monster movie, a giant Mercury Island tusked weta looms over all other invertebrates on the forest floor. Its tusks — two and a half centimetres long and borne only by males — are used in fighting.

Top right: Two male tusked weta fight for supremacy. The engagement involves a great deal of pushing and shoving in a test of strength and stamina. Each male twists his head in an attempt to flip his opponent on his back.

Bottom right: A giant weta species recently discovered in the Paparoa Range is the giant mole weta. This unusual insect burrows underground. Its hind legs are heavily armoured and used as spiky "gates" to block the entrance of its burrow.

Above: Looking more like a hedgehog from Mars than a New Zealand invertebrate, this tiny creature is a flightless giant in its own right. The *Collembola*, or springtails, are minuscule hopping litter dwellers that aid greatly in breaking down dead leaves to release nutrients. The orange-spined collembolan cannot hop or spring, however, despite being, at almost a centimetre in length, the largest springtail in the world.

Top right: The tiny moss weta, a relative of the cave weta, hides among the umbrella moss of the West Coast forest floor. New Zealand's only green weta, moss weta are common and widespread in the South Island, though seldom seen and as yet possessing no scientific name.

Right: A wingless kelp fly strides spider-like over the leaf of a sub-antarctic megaherb in the Antipodes Islands. Such wingless flies are a common feature of many of New Zealand's subantarctic islands.

New Zealand boasts a remarkable 30 species of stick insect, all of them flightless, some of them giants. A twig-like male Hutton's stick insect mates with a large female on a fern frond (*above*), while a male spiny stick insect mates with his larger, green partner on a pohutukawa flower (*left*). For many other New Zealand stick insect species, no males have ever been found; the females seem to reproduce asexually, laying eggs that hatch into identical young in spring (*bottom left*).

Giant flightless weevils were once widespread throughout New Zealand. A pair of knobbled weevils mate on an *Anisotome* leaf on Breaksea Island off the coast of Fiordland (*top right*), while a speargrass weevil forages on another *Anisotome* species in the Gertrude Valley, Fiordland (*right*). These and many other large flightless beetles today are confined either to offshore islands or to "ecological islands" high in the mountains on the mainland, where they are safe from the depredation of rats.

ON A WING AND A PRAYER

CHAPTER SEVEN

A NEW ISLAND VOLCANO IS BORN.   It emerges, hissing and gurgling, from a seafloor vent in the vast Pacific Ocean. Soon it is cool enough to receive life, but what sort of life? Successful colonisation will depend very much on species' ability to travel either by water or by air. Dispersal is a fundamental biological function.

Sea birds, without doubt, will be the first visitors to the new island. Among them will be found the supertramps of dispersal. Albatrosses may in one week travel from the east coast of Australia across the Pacific to feeding grounds off Tierra del Fuego. Having the west wind at their backs certainly helps.

On any day in most parts of the southern ocean, far from land, there will be sea birds, but what else is likely to be out there. How about a small, noisy flock of parakeets? It is true. Kakariki, the red-crowned parakeet, is an expert disperser. Populations were once to be found from Tahiti to Maquarie Island and on most islands in between. Having landed on a new island, they will eat anything from nectar and insects to seeds and leaves. They do not seem to mind if no trees grow on their adopted home, and have been known to make do on dead penguins and limpets. They are pioneering parrots that have probably been regularly colonising New Zealand from Australia since before the ice ages. It is likely that ancestors of the plucky red crown from Australia gave rise to all four species of parakeet in New Zealand.

Trans-Tasman colonisation of New Zealand, aided by the westerlies, has been a very well-used avenue of dispersal for millions of years, and is still being used. Shoveller ducks, silvereyes, spur-winged plovers and welcome swallows have all colonised from Australia within historical times. Recently a small flock of silvereyes was seen from a ship 600 kilometres east of New Zealand. Who knows where they were going? The Pacific Ocean is a vast body of water and most islands are correspondingly small. Dispersal is a chancy business.

Above the Tasman Sea, high over the waves and the sea birds, other, smaller travellers may sometimes be found. Moths, butterflies and a varied assortment of insects are regularly carried across the

A red-crowned parakeet, seemingly a long way from home, is perfectly at ease in a papaya tree in New Caledonia. This one-time traveller has spread into the subtropical Pacific as far as French Polynesia, as well as south to our own subantarctic islands.

1,200 kilometres of ocean on high, hot winds that blow out from the Australian desert. These same winds also bring to New Zealand uncountable millions of tiny spores and the light-as-air seeds of pioneering plants. Most are unsuccessful in finding new sites to colonise, but there have been times when New Zealand, like a new volcano thrust up out of the Pacific Ocean, has offered marvellous opportunities for pioneering plants, which have claimed new land in the name of Flora.

AGE BEFORE BEAUTY   Over time, regular trans-Tasman fliers have included spores of the ancients — lichens, mosses, lycopods and ferns. Among these are plants whose ancestors ruled the world. Great forests of cycads, club mosses, horsetails and ferns covered the Earth during the Devonian period over 300 million years ago. Today, most surviving species exist as small, damp-loving specimens without lofty pretensions. The only ancients to keep their heads held high are the tree ferns.

Tree ferns are pioneers. It is they who quickly claim the space created when a forest giant falls. The ancient tree fern has even formed an alliance with New Zealand's newest — introduced — tree, *Pinus radiata*. It can be seen flourishing beneath the open, well-pruned canopy of pine tree forest that lines the highway between Rotorua and Taupo. Given adequate moisture, tree ferns will clothe roadsides, hillsides and gullies — wherever land has lost its vegetative cover. Rather than being reviled as weeds, tree ferns should be celebrated as stately protectors of injured Earth. Groves of mamaku, the giant tree fern, clothe the regenerating slopes of many hills and gullies. But no matter where they grow, these pure stands are temporary. As young forest trees rise up beneath them, the tree ferns' spores are already blowing away to open space and a new home.

Tree ferns have a secret. They are not trees at all, their trunks being neither living nor woody. Simply, they comprise a large rosette fern sitting on top of a column made from its own dead frond bases and extensive fibrous root system. They are certainly tree-like, however, and on islands where there are no real trees they are perhaps better considered honorary trees for their role as forest makers. Several

127

other families of flowering plants boast members that have learnt the same trick. Even small herbs can evolve into substantial trees when the opportunity arises.

FIRST IN FIRST SERVED   Seeds that arrive on the wind in a new land do not have to face immigration control. Islands accept whatever long-distance dispersers happen to blow in, and that often means weeds. Weeds are staunch pioneers. Their lightweight seeds land and germinate in open spaces to grow into herbs or, at most, small shrubs.

About 28 million years ago, a new, weedy family of flowering plants began to parachute seeds into New Zealand. The timing was perfect because although the land was low lying and forested, it soon became restless and was rent asunder by uplift and earthquake. These ructions created bare surfaces — perfect conditions for the new family of herbs and shrubs to spread rapidly. Later, as the Southern Alps began to rise, the immigrants found their true calling. The family is of course the *Compositae*, the daisy family, and now more than 100 species of all shapes, sizes and genera live in the mountains of New Zealand. In venturing into the hills, the family has overcome tremendous obstacles. Daisies, by and large, are annual plants that die off in winter and regrow in spring, but the mountain daisies have evolved not to die off but to thicken their leaves and stems so that they can resist winter and in some cases endure a prolonged smothering by deep snow.

The champion daisies of the mountains are those of the *Celmisia* genus, which accounts for half of all the species found up there. Others, such as vegetable sheep and scab weeds, have become highly specialised, but no daisies, wherever they grow or whatever they do, have forgotten their pioneering spirit. Every summer they all put up their characteristic flowers, each flower being actually a tight group of many flowers. After fertilisation these "flowers within flowers" dry and squadrons of seeds on parachutes are sent away on the breeze to colonise new surfaces.

Some members of the daisy family have experimented successfully with the tree form. As New Zealand's blanket of forests has tended to suppress upstart herbs or shrubs from masquerading as trees, the daisies have confined their experiments generally to the mountains or to offshore islands. The most successful genus of tree daisies is without doubt *Olearia*. Many of its 30 or more species are trees or, at the very least, woody shrubs. Some form broad and impenetrable zones on mountainsides above the "real" forests. Trampers will vouch for the thick-leaved, stout-stemmed, uncompromising resistance of leatherwood, tupare or muttonbird scrub, as *Olearia colensoi* is variously known throughout the length of the land.

ONCE UPON AN ISLAND   New Zealand's offshore islands are a mere scatter of dots over a vast ocean between subtropics and subantarctic. Their generally equable climate and reliable rainfall have provided providential conditions for many pioneering plants whose seeds have flown or sailed to their far-

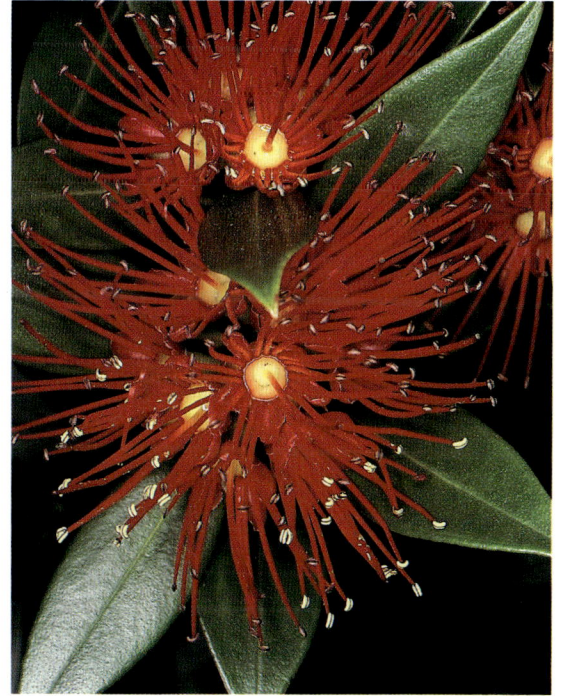

Right: New Zealand's mountain daisies are large and spectacular members of the alpine flora. They have occupied every available niche in the mountains and come in a variety of sizes and shapes, from creeping mat plants to woody shrubs.

Far right: *Metrosideros* species also vary, from spectacular forest trees with scarlet blooms, such as this southern rata, to shrubs and vines with orange, yellow or white flowers.

flung shores. Daisies feature among the flying pioneers on some, although not all, of these islands. On the Snares Islands the forest consists entirely of tree daisies.

The canopy is dominated, naturally enough, by an *Olearia*, which covers three-quarters of the main island. The large, leathery, fuzz-covered leaves of *Olearia lyalli* are so strong that a single leaf easily supports the weight of a roosting sea bird. The other tree daisy present is a giant *Senecio* (from Latin *senex*, old man — a reference to the white hairs on its seed). *Senecio stewartiae* is a beautiful, yellow-flowered, small tree that grows in valleys mostly on the eastern side of the islands. Tree daisies thrive here, despite their roots being riddled with muttonbird burrows. The only place where the forest dies is amid the muddy, filthy, nitrogen-overloaded patches of ground where Snares crested penguins have established colonies.

One possible reason for the success of daisies in forming the forest of the Snares has been lack of competition from other plants. The island supports just 20 species of flowering plant and none of these is a woody tree. The daisies can never be anything more than small trees because they are genetically programmed for smallness, but they can make wood. Saw through an arm-thick branch of any of them and the daisy's abilities will be revealed. There is wood, laid down in annual rings from a single wood-producing layer called the cambium, just like a forest giant in miniature.

Four hundred and fifty kilometres south of New Zealand grow trees that have affinities to forest giants yet belong to a genuine pioneering family. On the lower eastern slopes of the Auckland Islands, sheltered from the blast of the winds of the Furious Fifties, grows a stunted forest dominated by southern rata. There is nothing remarkable to be seen beneath the canopy among its iron-hard branches except for the occasional adventurous sea lion pup or perhaps a homecoming yellow-eyed penguin. Up above is where this southerly member of an amazing pioneering family wears its floral

129

badge of distinction. In summer the trees blaze scarlet with nectar-rich flowers, much to the delight of the local bellbirds. Flowers of this design, composed of a "brush" of bright red stamens around the margin of a glistening nectar-filled cup, identify *Metrosideros* wherever they are found. Later in the summer their unique qualities are again evident. After fertilisation the ovaries beneath the flower cups swell and then burst, releasing vast numbers of seeds that are carried like dust in the air. Members of the genus *Metrosideros* are among the very few large trees of the world that have such a liberal attitude to dispersal.

Rata and their like are flying pioneers. Sometimes their flowers are yellow, but most often it is a blazing canopy of red that identifies them throughout their range. Some are parasites, others are stragglers. They are found throughout the Pacific from Hawaii in the north to the Marquesas in the east and as far south as the Auckland Islands. Wherever they grow, however, none matches the size, form and grandeur of *Metrosideros excelsa*, New Zealand's pohutukawa.

Pohutukawa is New Zealand's own Christmas tree and the distinguishing feature of northern coastlines, where its pioneering abilities are the stuff of legend. On Rangitoto Island in the Waitemata Harbour, pohutukawa established themselves on the knobbly black lava soon after the island's eruption 700 years ago. Windblown seeds that established themselves in light, moist crevices put down long, tortuous roots and, later, extended clusters of small shoots. These seedlings have now grown up to become trees of life on Rangitoto. Their shoots have become giant, radiating branches that provide shade, food and moisture for a variety of other plants whose seeds have either blown or hitchhiked to the young island.

Among the plant immigrants sheltering beneath pohutukawa's welcoming arms are orchids and over 100 species of moss and liverwort, plants well known for their airborne dispersing abilities. Here, too, are other familiar flying pioneers for whom the journey to Rangitoto was a breeze.

Of the 40 species of fern that grow mainly in shady glades on Rangitoto, the most distinctive are New Zealand's unique kidney ferns. Out closer to the margin of the life-giving shade provided by pohutukawa grows the walking fern, *Asplenium flabellifolium*. Wherever its fronds touch the ground, new plantlets form, and in this way it "walks" across the lava. Many perching plants, or epiphytes, that live high in the branches of mainland New Zealand forests are seen to perch on the ground out on Rangitoto Island. Among these down-to-earth types are ferns and one of the most attractive flowering plants in the entire flora of New Zealand. Its beautiful cascading blooms are those of a daisy. It is called kahurangi, or mist of the skies, and on Rangitoto it comes to earth, along with the ferns, beneath the splendid pohutukawa. These three airborne pioneers have made a unique claim on New Zealand's youngest island.

Left: Nature's red mantle unfurls as the first of the flowering pohutukawa trees on the Poor Knights Islands begin to burst into bloom. In a couple more weeks a crimson canopy will extend to the horizon as this pioneering tree supplies an abundance of food for all the reptiles concealed within its forest. Pohutukawa is a remarkable tree, the seeds of which can disperse on the wind and are capable of germinating on bare rock.

Above: The fallen crimson leaves and scarlet flowers of another *Metrosideros*, the southern rata, grace the umbrella moss floor of a West Coast rainforest.

Above: Looking more like a woolly rock than a plant, a large, mat-forming vegetable sheep "bursts" into flower, its tiny yellow blossoms giving no more than the faintest blush to its wool-like foliage.

Right: The black scree daisy soaks up the alpine sun on a Canterbury scree slope, its tiny composite flower head easily overlooked by all but the mountain butterflies that pollinate it.

Far right: A closely related species blooms at the edge of a Marlborough scree slope.

A rare, carnivorous bat-winged fly, with black pantalooned wings, alights on a large-flowered mat daisy, a relative of the vegetable sheep.

Left: A Snares crested penguin nests beneath a flowering Stewart Island tree daisy.
Far left: A closely related tree daisy in bloom in the Chatham Islands.
Above: The Snares Islands forests are composed entirely of two daisy species. No other forest trees have reached the Snares. Such an extraordinary forest is made even more remarkable by the occasional presence of a perching penguin.

Forests of soft tree ferns typical of the great fern forests of the past are still to be found growing in many wet gullies in New Zealand (*right*). Tree fern trunks often provide the base from which *Tmesipteris* can sprout (*above left*), a tiny primitive fern ally seen here producing its spore capsules amongst the mosses, liverworts and filmy ferns which festoon the tree fern trunk. Many of these plants bear packets of spores which are light and easily dispersed by wind and water, such as those arranged in neat patches on the underside of a hound's tongue fern frond (*top left*). The boldly textured black tree fern trunk (*above right*) isn't really a trunk in the real sense, just the dead woody stem of the fern, atop which the rosette of the living fern perches.

AGAINST THE FLOW

CHAPTER EIGHT

THERE IS NOTHING QUITE LIKE A WHITEBAIT FRITTER, especially one from the West Coast. First, West Coast fritters are huge and contain a lot more whitebait than batter. Second, the whitebait from the Coast are bigger than those caught elsewhere in New Zealand. Why this should be is only one of the many mysteries that surround these little fish that swim in from the sea and up into the rivers in uncountable numbers.

The whitebait run is as much part of spring on the Coast as the arrival of the kotuku, the white heron, prior to breeding. These elegant birds enact their annual ritual of courting, nest building, egg laying and chick rearing up in the branches of trees that overhang the river. Below them the whitebait run, day after day, week after week, like a stream within a stream, against the flow, towards the mountains.

The run begins with the first spring flood. Snow melt in the Southern Alps combines with heavy rain on the Coast to sluice great plumes of fresh water out into the Tasman Sea. Each river colours the ocean according to its origin. The biggest fans of colour spread out from rock-flour grey, snow-fed rivers. The smaller, local forest catchments add their characteristic tannin browns. On the surface, far beyond the tumbling breakers, a ragged line of foam marks the boundary between fresh and salt water. Below, denser, colder river water slides out beyond the boundary to lose its identity in powerful currents that sweep along the coast.

Fresh and salt water mix in a zone where the five species of larval fish known collectively as whitebait come together. It is like a vast railway station filled with tiny, ghost-like refugees. Apart from eye dots, the translucent bodies of the bait render them invisible. All have ceased eating as part of the preparation for the journey ahead. Like a railway station, the river offers different destinations. Some whitebait are attracted to the clearer, icy waters that flow directly from the mountains. Others, such as the golden bait of the giant kokopu, will seek out the acid taste of the brown-stained forest rivers later in the season. The most common of the bait species is the slightly green-hued young inanga; this is also the least selective in its choice of destination. It forms 95 per cent of the whitebait in most West Coast rivers.

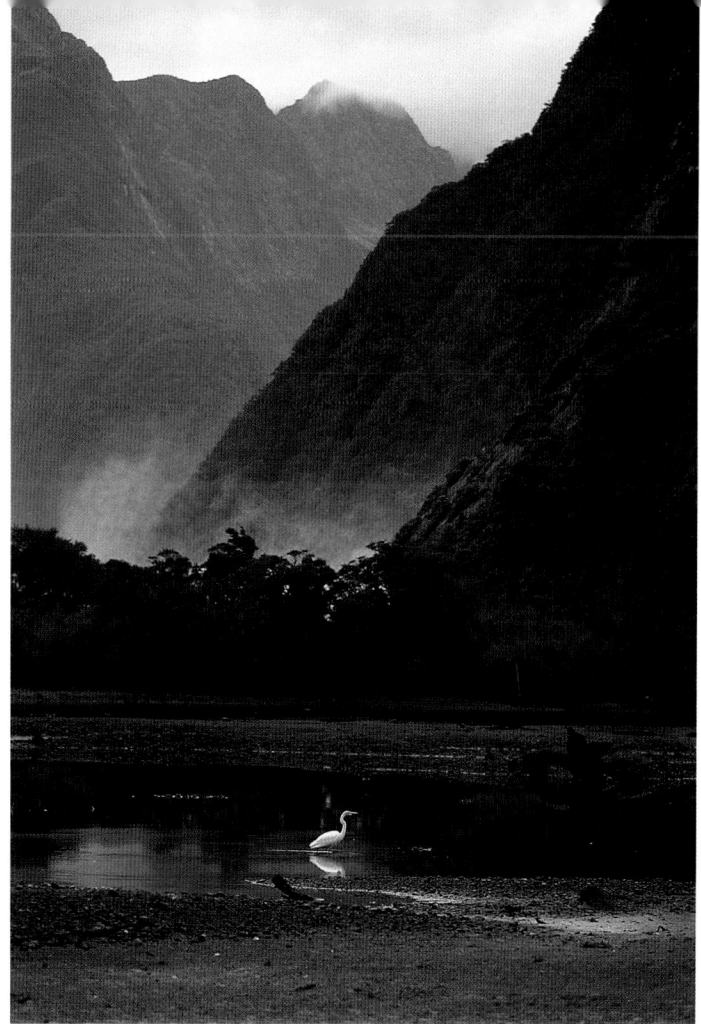

Early morning at Milford Sound — and like any good whitebaiter a lone white heron stands and waits for the return of the "run", a term used to describe the seasonal migration of larval galaxiid fish.

Long before the slow train of whitebait reaches the rivermouth it is ambushed. At first just a few stray silver bullets burst through the school, but soon the sea surface boils with gorging kahawai. Yet the little fish swim onwards — inexorable, unstoppable. Their journey to the river is an extension of a much greater journey that began in another time in the waters around the supercontinent of Gondwana. Whitebait are juveniles of an ancient genus of southern hemisphere freshwater fish called *Galaxias*. Following the great wrenching apart of Gondwana, some species developed such that they remained in one area while others dispersed round the southern ocean to inhabit rivers in South Africa, Australia, Lord Howe Island, New Caledonia, New Zealand, South America and the Falkland Islands. Part of the survival strategy — and the mystery — of galaxiids has been their diadromous behaviour, according to which they spend one part of their growing lives at sea and the other part where they were born and will probably die, in fresh water.

Within the mouths of rivers and estuaries along the West Coast awaits another suite of predators. At the head of Milford Sound a juvenile white heron, not yet old enough to join the breeding colony, stabs half-heartedly at whitebait that advance up the small rivulet in which she stands. Having already had her fill she continues hunting more out of habit and for distraction. The silver stream of fish parts, swirls around the heron's gnarled legs and reunites itself to push on against the flow.

The thick rope flexes up and over a block and tackle. A lone fisherman on a rickety jetty hauls up a large box net. Water cascades from the complicated arrangement of traps and partitions. Pulling a

139

Its tiny face picked out in a galaxy of black stars, New Zealand's commonest galaxiid, an adult inanga (*above left*), faces upstream watching for food. The giant kokopu (*above right*), the largest of all our galaxiid species, once grew to nearly 60 centimetres in length and weighed two and a half to three kilograms — true giants of their kind. Sadly, such large individuals are now very uncommon. Today these dark, chocolate-brown fish are usually to be found only in deep, still, peaty streams and lakes (*right*), where they conceal themselves amongst the flax by day.

lever releases about a kilogram of writhing silver into a plastic bucket. Although there are many more nets suspended below many more jetties, the estuary is broad and innumerable whitebait elude these unseen traps to run yet another gauntlet of predators. From dark waterways below, eels insinuate themselves into their midst, and shags beat their wings in underwater pursuit of this annual bounty. From above, gulls swoop and kingfishers dive. That there are sufficient whitebait to survive such a massacre in the estuary is due to an event that took place here six months ago.

At that time the estuary seemed to overflow. The autumn full moon, which made the reflections of giant kahikatea wriggle on the water, had brought this very high tide. It was also the signal that brought millions of the 20-centimetre-long adult inanga, *Galaxias maculatus*, out of nearby rivers and streams to spawn. Their densely patterned bodies gleam like a galaxy of stars, which accounts for the name *Galaxias* being given to this ancient group of freshwater fish. The shallow pools and puddles around the estuary margin became white with the males' milt as they writhed around the swollen females that swam among the grasses and flax. At the very height of the tide of the full moon, each female laid masses of eggs, which looked like clumps of sago, at the base of the vegetation. During the next two weeks, life surged within these millions of eggs. Development, as always, was timed for hatching to occur at the next high tide, which would come with the new moon. Two weeks later the tides came but were not high enough to cover the plants, and the minute larvae were forced to wait, developmentally suspended within their egg chambers. Another two weeks brought another full moon. This time the tides were high enough for water to lap around the stems of the estuary plants that were festooned with egg masses. A brief immersion is all it took to trigger the hatching and mobilisation of

a transcendent mass of comma-sized baby inanga. The moon, the tide, the river — all acted in concert to sweep the tiny travellers out to sea, on the first stage of a great adventure. That adventure has now brought them back, against the flow, half a year later.

A DUCK OUT OF WATER?   The dark, iridescent shape of a male blue duck (or whio) flies low and hard for a short distance down a forest-lined West Coast river. It banks steeply and repeats the aerial reconnaissance upstream. This is his twice-daily routine, at dawn and dusk. Having satisfied himself that all is well and that there are no other waterfowl to chase from his 1 kilometre stretch of riverside territory, he alights in a pool beside the rapids. He calls his mate of four seasons, who is holding station in the swirling confusion of white water. She has been minding their week-old chicks. Not that these four require much baby-sitting. They bounce like fluffy corks in the fiercest surges of the rapids. Beneath the surface, their oversized feet propel them furiously yet confidently away from danger.

The splayed branches of beech trees almost touch above midstream, and the banks are dense with grasses and shrubs along this stretch of the river. The water hurries on its course, shaded into a perpetual twilight which brings the rocks to life. Low-slung, wriggling bodies cling to the tops and downstream surfaces of the boulders. They are the nymphs and larvae of mayflies, caddis flies, stoneflies, bugs, beetles and other photosensitive insects that come out of hiding in the gloom of the overhanging vegetation. These insects are the staple diet of the young galaxiid fish that continue their journey upstream, unseen, close to the riverbank.

The carnivorous blue ducks also rely on the insects on the rocks. While her chicks watch, the mother begins to feed. She moves into position in the downstream eddy of a large boulder. Her head dips below the surface. The insects are quickly scooped and sucked off their rock with the aid of the membranous flanges on the margin of her bill. The process is repeated. Occasionally she uses her strong feet to grip the riverbed as she harvests the wriggling crop off a boulder in the rapids.

In many New Zealand rivers, blue duck are frequently beaten to this harvest by a most efficient introduced predator. Brown trout have grown fat on stream insects, a development which has played a large part in excluding blue duck from many river systems. Forest clearance has further reduced their numbers by destroying the specific riverside conditions that blue duck require.

Other ducks have divided up the waterways of New Zealand between them. Some, such as mallard, grey duck and the teal species, pursue a mixed diet of plants, seeds and invertebrates strained from the mud of slow rivers, lakes and wetlands. Scaup dive to hunt animal prey mainly in lakes. Paradise shelduck have benefited most from human manipulation of habitat, pairs of shelduck now ranging far and wide over pasture. Yet the highly territorial blue duck, the species we assume to be the most restricted in its watery needs, may also once have roamed far and wide. There is evidence that it foraged deep into the forests that once covered much of this land in a continuous blanket of diversity and munificence.

The presence of many blue duck fossil bones at several sites near Nelson has placed these birds in a forest environment many kilometres from their riverside territories. Their remains have even been found out on exposed ridges. It is not difficult to imagine them fossicking for invertebrates in the rich layer of leaf litter of prehuman New Zealand forests. There was food for all there. It is now known that rails and a number of wading birds took on lifestyles away from the swamp, feeding instead on the riches of the forest floor. So why could not this most ancient and unique of waterfowl have become, at times, a duck out of water? Trampers and hunters still report the occasional blue duck in the forest far from the nearest river.

A FISH OUT OF WATER   Of the five species of young galaxiid that come in through the rivermouths of New Zealand only one can find it's way to the headwaters of icy, snow-fed rivers. Koaro are also called climbing galaxiids, owing to a unique ability among their kind which allows them to negotiate weirs, rapids and even waterfalls. A school of koaro gathers in olive-green confusion at the base of a mighty obstacle, the concrete face of a small hydroelectric dam. On some rivers fish ladders offer finned

The koaro is one of several species of galaxiid fish which make up the whitebait run. Adult koaro possess the extraordinary ability of leaving the water if the going gets tough and climbing over wet rocks, using their pelvic fins as limbs, rather than swimming against a strong current.

migrants assisted passage upriver. On others, such as this one, there is no assistance for migrating fish. Hydroelectric schemes are but one of many problems for native fish to overcome. Others include the clearance of 85 per cent of lowland forest, the draining of 90 per cent of wetlands, and competition from and predation by 20 species of introduced freshwater fish. Having all this to contend with, a concrete wall should be a pushover for the finger-length koaro.

Rather than be forced back by the power of the spillway, the climbing galaxiids haul themselves out of the water and ascend the damp concrete splash zone to one side. Their climbing technique relies on suction. Small ridges on the underside of their pectoral fins form a series of suckers when applied to the damp surface. Fin over fin they climb, using the ventral surfaces of their bodies as another suction cup. At last the obstacle is cleared and they are able to proceed into the tussock-fringed rivers above the lake. Here they will live out their lives in modest yet determined competition with those most successful of finned imports, brown trout.

Closer still to the mountains there is to be found yet another galaxiid. The Alpine galaxiid, *Galaxias paucispondylus*, inhabits the highly oxygenated mountain streams to the east of the Southern Alps. It is one of eight species that do not go to sea every year. Theirs is an entirely river-based existence. Native galaxiids are to be found in waterways from sea level to mountain altitudes and from dry mud ponds to tumbling rapids. All have travelled against the flow, either in their own lifetime or in the ancient migration of their ancestors across the ocean to form a vital part of New Zealand's native fish fauna.

Above: A pair of blue duck escort their three downy chicks upstream. Subfossil evidence suggests that this species once ranged widely through the forests as well as along waterways.
Right: A male New Zealand scaup dives to the bottom of a clear South Island hydroelectric lake. A true diving duck, the scaup can propel itself to considerable depths in search of prey on the lakebed.
Far right: A female paradise shelduck stands like a lone sentinel in a High Country basin. These grazing birds have benefited from the clearance of agricultural land throughout the country.

The brown teal, once a common denizen of swamps and waterways throughout New Zealand, is all but extinct on the mainland because of predation by introduced mammals.

Three shield shrimps swim amongst waterweed in an ephemeral pond (*above*). These extraordinary crustaceans find it very difficult to compete with pond dwellers in permanent waters, and are only to be found in temporary ponds and puddles in summer. Other invertebrate inhabitants of the shield shrimps' ponds include the carnivorous larvae of the delicate blue damselfly (*top right*), as well as the more robust larvae of larger dragonflies (*above right*).

Living treasures found on South Island broad-braided riverbeds are easily overlooked. Rounded river stones patterned with crustose lichen nestle in a bed of South Island edelweiss (*top near right*), while a robust grasshopper, the most endangered of our short-horned grasshoppers, perches atop a river boulder (*top far right*).

Beautifully camouflaged to merge with the river stones, two eggs (*right*) lie waiting for their owner to return (*above*). The New Zealand wrybill is a specialist of these High Country rivers. With its sideways curved beak, bent always to the right, it is another unusual product of New Zealand's avian evolution.

THE HILLS ARE ALIVE

CHAPTER NINE

OBLIVIOUS OF ONE OF THE FINEST VIEWS TO BE HAD anywhere in New Zealand, a grasshopper with a hairy back munches hungrily on the fluffy petals of a prostrate herb on the sunny side of Mount Enys, the highest peak in the Craigieburn Range. To the west the Southern Alps are etched in sparkling clarity, cleansed by a passing storm which still rumbles away eastward, darkening the distant Pacific Ocean.

Like the warming sun, the grasshopper has not long emerged from its hiding place, following five days of storm-bound concealment. Snow fills the hollows and depressions. There are few plants up here, which is hardly surprising, at an altitude of more than 2,000 metres. The plant with the woolly flower is *Leucogenes grandiceps*, or the South Island edelweiss. Though named for its similarity to edelweiss of the Swiss Alps, it is a member of the daisy family. The hairy grasshopper is *Sigaus villosus*, the most high-alpine of the 11 species of mountain grasshopper.

A green-brown bird with brilliant red underwings lands gently on a nearby emergent rock. The grasshopper panics and leaps away onto a bank of soft snow. Then something remarkable happens. Instead of floundering about in the snow, the grasshopper "skis" away downslope. Using its hind legs as poles and its smooth, ribbed abdomen as a ski, it makes excellent progress over to some rocks. This extraordinary behaviour gives *Sigaus villosus* its nickname — Skiing Siggy. However, it isn't just Skiing Siggy's ability as a downhill racer which is unusual — so is its very presence up here. Skiing Siggy is a short-horned grasshopper and belongs to a large group more commonly represented in the tropics. Its most famous (or perhaps infamous) relation is the locust. The bird on the rock and the plant on which the grasshopper was feeding also seem out of place in the mountains.

The bird uses its long, curved beak to nibble the centre out of a yellow flower that looks uncannily like a buttercup. It *is* a buttercup, named *Ranunculus crithmifolius* and discovered by J.D. Enys, after whom this mountain is named. Buttercups usually belong near streams or bogs. The bird is a kea, a parrot — and parrots belong in noisy flocks either in tropical rainforests or in the heat of the

Sigaus villosus, the hairy grasshopper, is the highest-dwelling of New Zealand's short-horned grasshoppers. No stranger to snow it even skis, hence its nickname — Skiing Siggy.

Australian outback. It would seem that the plant, the bird and the grasshopper are all a very long way from home.

FIRST FLOOR, GOING UP It is uncertain whether the mountains of the Southern Alps of New Zealand are rising at a continuous rate or in a series of stop-start episodes, the equivalent of pausing at each floor in an elevator. One thing is certain, however — they are rising, and their ascent from flat, warm land to steep, cold mountains began in earnest about five million years ago. What is more, it is generally understood that grasshoppers, buttercups, parrots and many of the other plants and animals found up here have risen with the Southern Alps.

No alps would be complete without yodelling, and New Zealand alps do have their yodellers. They are a species of an ancient line of plant-juice-sucking insects called cicadas. Sir Charles Fleming, who gave *Maoricicada clamitans* the name the yodelling cicada, must have had a lively imagination. Out on a subalpine shrub, to the south of the rampaging, snow-fed Rangitata River, a male cicada "yodels" with full voice, sounding more like a set of punctured bagpipes than a lederhosen-clad Austrian from the Tyrol. He produces his irresistible (to a female cicada) sound by using powerful muscles to buckle the ribbed, flexible membranes, or tymbals, on either side of his body. The yodel is amplified through resonating chambers in other parts of his black, cigar-shaped abdomen.

151

Each species of cicada has a distinct song, which can be a useful guide to identification. In fact males of the closely related *Maoricicada cassiope*, found just to the north of the Rangitata River, have a most unyodel-like song — they shriek. What separated the yodeller and the shrieker was the Ice Age, which descended upon New Zealand as well as most of the rest of the world. It came and went in four stages of glacial advance and retreat, beginning almost two million years ago and closing with the reversal of the most recent ice advance approximately 10,000 years ago. At the height of each glacial period, a vast cap of ice sat on top of the growing alps, spreading vast glaciers to the east and west. This massive cooling of New Zealand's South Island forced plant and animal, friend and foe, to cling to the margins of ice-free land that were to be found in the north near Nelson and in the southern pockets of Fiordland and Otago. The isolating effect of the Ice Age provides the answer to how the kea, the alpine grasshoppers and perhaps even the buttercups came to develop a lifestyle in the mountains and how the shrieking and yodelling cicadas came to sound so distinctly different.

All that yodelling has paid off. It has served to attract a nearby female. Following copulation she flies away downslope to lay her eggs. She prepares her egg nest by making a cut with her ovipositor in the woody stem of a dragon tree, *Dracophyllum pronum*. Further downslope the whole hillside ripples golden as the wind plays with the snow tussock, *Chionocloa rigida*.

A COOL FASHION "Merino wethers," said the boss to the young shepherd, "can live way up on the tops for months and bloody near all they need to keep themselves going is the view."

The merinos may well enjoy the view, but they also enjoy chomping a fair number of the more than 500 native plant species found in the High Country. Ninety per cent of these plants do not grow anywhere else in the world. The move up with the mountains proved most popular with several plant families in particular. The genus *Hebe*, for which New Zealand is botanically well known far and wide, comprises one third of all the commoner alpine shrubs. Alpine plants are not wimps. They can survive frost, violent wind and also snow, which may lie over them for months. The soil in which they grow is often frozen, which means their roots are unable to extract nutrients. Soil also disintegrates when ice forms and again when it melts. Finally, alpine plants must be able to withstand sudden changes in climate.

A lazy wind blows across the spur where the shepherd works his dogs. It is a lazy wind because it doesn't blow round him; instead it cuts straight through. On this bitterly cold, clear autumn day, the moving mass of white in the distance progresses downslope at the urging of the dogs, constantly changing shape like an amoeba.

Out on a small, rocky ridge a few sheep stand their ground defiantly. The shepherd sends a dog back to bring them into the moving flock. Still the sheep stand motionless. Through binoculars the young shepherd sees his mistake. These are not merinos. He has been the victim of one of the High Country's oldest botanical hoaxes. He has just attempted to muster a small flock of vegetable sheep. These extra-

The most spectacular of all alpine blooms belong to the giant buttercup known as the Mount Cook lily, the large white flowers of which are typical of the either white or yellow blooms which characterise so many alpine flowering plants in New Zealand.

ordinary shrubs are daisies but are quite unlike any that grow in the front garden. Up close, the broad, white mass that covers the rock can be seen to be a smooth, hard "shell" or mat of tightly packed woolly leaves all of the same length. Beneath this solid botanical barrier a multitude of branches converge on a single stem and to a long root that penetrates deep into the fractured rock. Also beneath the foliage is a peaty deposit made up of the plant's own decaying leaves and branchlets, which acts like blotting paper to retain water. With its hard shell to protect it from the extremes of heat and cold, a vegetable sheep, when not being mistaken for an errant merino, might well appear more like a solar-powered crash helmet than a plant.

The mountains support a cohort of mat plants, each similar in design to the vegetable sheep but belonging to very different families. This growth form is popular among *Raoulia*, *Donatia* and *Hectorella*. These rugged types do have a softer side, however. In summer, their hard shells sprout a profusion of minute white or yellow flowers. Despite their tough exteriors, they are all just flowering plants at heart.

New Zealand's native flower garden is to be found not among the dappled greenery of its forest trees but up in the mountains. Flowering begins even before the spring snow melt, with the white buds of *Caltha*, and continues in a wonderful procession of blooms right through summer, until the gentians mark the season's end. Appreciation of New Zealand's alpine flowers depends on a particular fondness for two colours — white and yellow — that attract the broadest range of pollinating insects both by day and during the night shift. The most spectacular bloom belongs to the giant buttercup, *Ranunculus lyalli*, which was named the Mount Cook lily in a fit of colonial confusion. Each of its many perfect flowers is made up of bold, white, overlapping petals. Even the plant itself seems most peculiarly bold and upright in an environment where most others keep their heads down. The leaves of the giant buttercup are huge and lush and seem more suited to a backyard pond, as a place for a frog to sit, than the freezing flanks of a mountain. The giant buttercup achieves such extravagance of form through the support and nurture of an extensive root system. The large leaves reciprocate by acting as formidable solar panels that in their short lifetime more than repay the roots their debt of sugary energy.

The harshness of the alpine climate has encouraged plants to don an almost universal cold-weather uniform of either hairy or woolly leaves that are leathery, thick and fleshy. A few of the hebes have taken the added step of mimicking the growth form of cypresses and pines, trees which specialise in mountain living. Their narrow branches are covered with scale-like leaves which give the appearance of whipcord. *Hebe cupressoides* is one that looks and smells like a cypress. The whipcord hebes are a celebration — or vindication — among flowering plants of the ecological adeptness of conifers.

A SECRET SOCIETY   Some years ago it was thought that the vast rock jumbles called screes that line many eastern faces of the Southern Alps were tangible evidence of excessive High Country burn-offs. Too many fires over too many years had created erosion scars of vast size and great frequency. "It was criminal," some said. Later, following close examination of the rind or coating of individual greywacke boulders within these rock falls, another story emerged. It has now been demonstrated that most scree slopes are surprisingly stable and many thousands of years old, and are in fact enduring evidence of massive erosion caused by the action of ice, water and wind on the rapidly rising mountains. Without erosion the Southern Alps, which have been growing at an average rate of 6 millimetres per year for almost five million years, would be twice the height of Mount Everest.

At first glance a scree slope is an untidy rock fall, spread precariously down an incline from which an avalanche would surely result. It appears arid, soilless and a most unsuitable place for plants or animals, yet both are found here. A select few plants and insects, found nowhere else, have become scree specialists. Together they form the secret society of scree dwellers. The plants are not seen at first because they are small, widely spread and the same grey colour as the rocks. Their fleshy leaves are very similar, yet their family origins are quite distinct.

A little black glider rides the microthermals above the scree. The black mountain butterfly lands near a few of the most visible of the plants, the black cotula. These plants mark the presence of a hidden stream, where a bizarre group of subterranean scavenging insects gathers. There are giant wingless stoneflies (*Holcoperla*) up to 4 centimetres long, giant grey and white weta with pink lapels (*Deinacrida connectans*) and weird carabid beetles. Theirs is an even more secret society than the plants'.

The most unusual scree bloom belongs to the penwiper, a relative of the humble cabbage. Its small, ivory-coloured flowers are set out on a massed head and emit a scent similar to that of stock, to which it is also related. Its name comes from the domed arrangement of its closely overlapping fleshy leaves, which are reminiscent of the sewn diamonds of felt on which quill pens were wiped of their excess ink.

The scree carrot (*Lignocarpa carnosula*), like most within the society, has an extensive root system, in this case a taproot. Below the rugged surface of the scree, stones graduate in size, becoming pro-

The kea is an unusual inhabitant of the South Island alpine region. It shares its mountain home with tussock-dwelling alpine grasshoppers and giant, spiky, flowering "carrots" (genus *Aciphylla*).

gressively smaller until damp, sandy silt is encountered at a depth of about 40 centimetres. The roots tap into moisture which seeps slowly downslope through the silt. Most scree plants have very thin stems which shear off and break easily in the event of a rock slide. A caterpillar waits to scavenge these decapitated plants, whose rootstock or rhizomes survive to sprout again. Such a strategy is preferable by far to risking total uprooting and death through having a stout stem.

The shepherd sets off a modest scree avalanche as he runs in a mad, striding dash that sees him 1,000 metres downslope in a little over two minutes. The merinos are already in the valley, heading to lower, winter pastures. The practice of grazing the "tops" is becoming rarer. More and more of this priceless habitat is being retired from sheep browsing and returned to its rightful browsers — the grasshoppers. Up on the scree another short-horned grasshopper munches another buttercup; this time it is the scree buttercup. Nearby the feathers of a young kea are ruffled by the first wind of another westerly front. There is snow in the air.

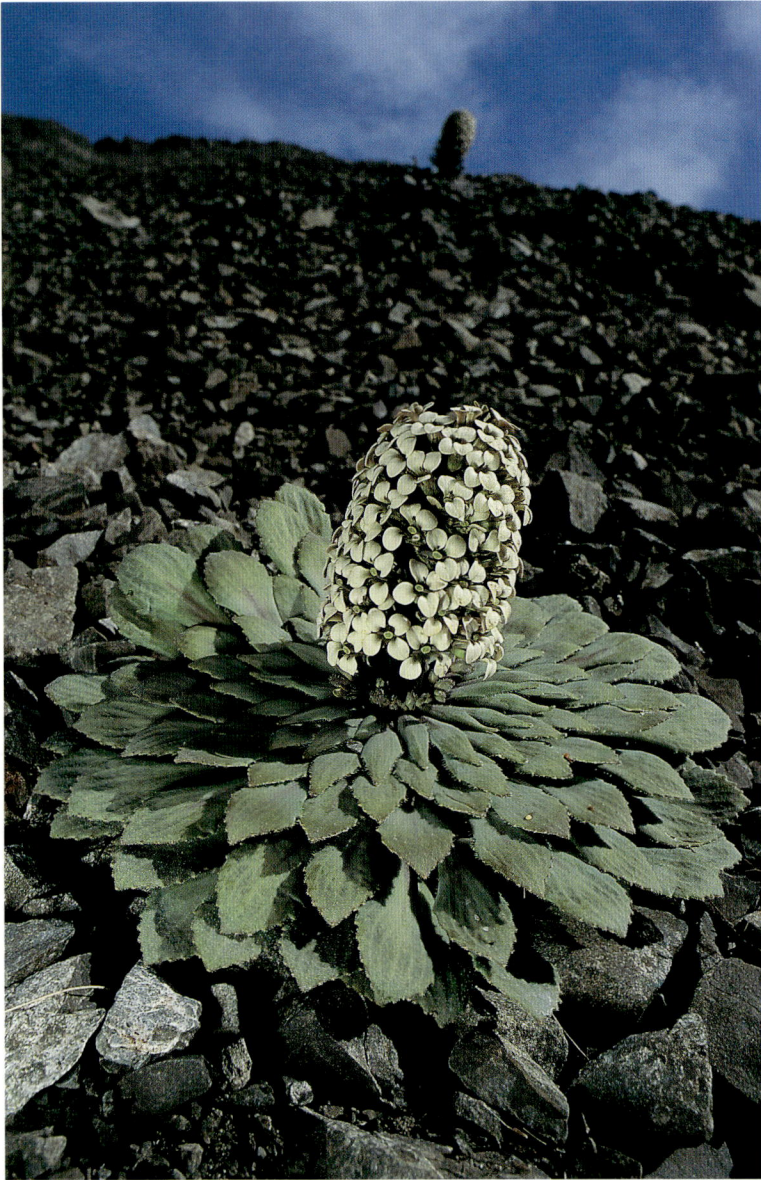

The penwiper (*above*) is just one of a number of unusual native plants to inhabit the dry scree slopes of the eastern South Island (*right*). Penwipers are members of the cabbage family. Their densely packed, overlapping leaves bear some resemblance to the overlapping felt mats used in Victorian times to wipe pen nibs clean, hence their name.

The scree slopes of the eastern South Island are home to a community of overlooked plants and secretive animals. Among them is the scree weta (*above left*), which feeds on *Hebe haastii*, a trailing, sprawling shrub with twisted branches that shares the highest recorded elevation for a vascular plant in New Zealand.

Above right: The same colour as the greywacke stones, a scree grasshopper stands partially camouflaged beside a mountain chickweed in full flower. The branching, succulent herb, too, has taken on the colour of the surrounding scree.

Above left: Nowhere else in the world do cicadas colonise such unfriendly habitats as the alpine environments of New Zealand. An alpine cicada sings from a bare rock on the scree.

Above right: A high-living alpine member of the daisy family, the South Island edelweiss displays its flowers, each petal entirely covered with a silvery-white wool.

Of the 15 species of short-horned grasshopper in New Zealand, 12 are limited to an alpine distribution, where they are significant browsers of High Country plants.
Above: Five colourful minute grasshoppers browse mat plants on an old river terrace in the Mackenzie Country, while (*right*) a black-eyed grasshopper from the Remarkables range stretches its legs in the alpine sun.

Above: A pair of tussock grasshoppers mate at the edge of a scree in the Seaward Kaikoura, the smaller male atop the female. Should danger threaten she will carry them both to safety.

Left: Scree grasshoppers are typically stone-grey. This pink individual at Porter's Pass probably derives its pigment from the bright red willowherb on which it feeds.

Top left: A poa tussock, surrounded by bare volcanic soil, grows on the North Island's central volcanic plateau.
New Zealand's tussock grasslands are home to a great variety of invertebrates. A common tussock butterfly (left) basks on an overcast day on an Otago snow tussock. A large flightless tussock weevil (above) sports the same colour and texture as the curled leaf bases of its tussock home in the Kaikoura mountains.

A field of the largest and most spectacular buttercups in the world, Mount Cook lilies (*above*), flower in profusion in Temple Basin at Arthur's Pass. Each spectacular plant produces panicles of white flowers from October through January. Although locally common along the side of streams, a field of Mount Cook lilies remains an unforgettable sight.

Alpine buttercups are conspicuous members of the alpine flora. Buchanan's buttercup (*top far right*) grows high up among the rocky clefts in the mountains of Fiordland. Korikori (*bottom near right*) prefers rock crevices in alpine tussock grasslands and herb fields from the East Cape in the North Island to the Kaikoura mountains in the South. The feathery-leaved buttercup (*bottom far right*) flowers in high, wet, rocky areas from Lewis Pass to Fiordland. Many of New Zealand's alpine hebes have adopted a whipcord growth habit. The cypress-like hebe (*top near right*) bears such a close resemblance to a cypress (it even smells like one) that a plant-sucking lice that specialises in feeding on alpine conifers has been fooled into feeding on the hebe instead. Once in flower, the hebe gives away its true nature, although its flowers are inconspicuous for its kind.

KILLER CLOWNS

CHAPTER TEN

A SLOW PROCESSION OF CARS FOLLOWS A DARK ZIGZAG through whiteness up to a sheltered basin in the mountain range aptly named the Remarkables.

By 9.00 a.m. the ski field car park is almost full. Car doors slam. Sunglasses mirror the grand vista of lake, toy town, farmscape and distant peaks. Heads swing back to take in the gently gliding chair lifts and the broad sweep of the beckoning slopes.

Other eyes, dark and knowing, observe the colourful confusion of the start of a day's skiing. Seven young kea sit perched on various vantage points. For them a sunny, winter Sunday means food and... an audience.

Lunch time is show time. Tired skiers watch as kea perform their latest juggling act. The first bird flies over the smiling, pointing crowd with a drink container in its beak and then drops it. As if from nowhere another kea intercepts the cup before it hits the ground, ascends and then also drops it. A third member of the troupe snatches the object out of the air and the routine is repeated many times, to the delight of the admiring throng. Meanwhile another pair play "king of the castle" on top of a plastic bucket, and a lone "peeping tom" looks into the men's loo through a skylight while hanging upside down from the spouting.

Kea are monkeys with feather cloaks. They delight in play and are lightning fast at picking up new tricks. They learn, as do monkeys and human children, through experiment and imitation. Just about everything about them is quite unparrot-like, but then no other parrot in the world lives where the kea makes its home — in the mountains.

The peaks that enclose the ski field are remarkable by nature as well as by name. From the west they rear up as an immense, jagged shield of schist rock. Snow sits in ancient scars and gouges inflicted by the mountain's Ice Age conflict with a massive glacier that flowed from the west. As the ice moulded the mountains, so it helped fashion the only mountain parrot in the world. Perhaps it has been the never-ending struggle to find food in this extreme environment which has further expanded this bird's intelligence and resourcefulness.

No other parrot in the world could survive in the icy wasteland of a kea's mountain home, yet the kea thrives and even plays here.

Small triangles of black rubber fall onto the white snow. They represent a considerable portion of the weather seal from around the windscreen of a late model four-wheel drive. The young perpetrator of this crime is a six-month-old kea. While one group entertains the ski set with tricks and games, others are vandalising their cars. Not that it is deliberate destruction. Young kea shred windscreen wipers and lever off chrome and wing mirrors as part of their adolescent search for truth, understanding and something edible. Ski field fixtures and fittings have now been rendered kea proof; cars have not. Having prised free another roof-rack pad, the young kea scrambles skyward, closely followed by a salvo of snowballs and a string of oaths. It is all part of our love-hate relationship with these incorrigible rogues. However, the vandalism they inflict on cars, tents, huts and other ski field installations is a minor misdemeanour compared to another crime of which kea stand accused. That crime is murder.

The same glacier that cut deep striations into the flanks of the Remarkables also gouged out the elongated S shape of Lake Wakatipu. It was here, amid the hills and valleys of Glenorchy at the western end of the lake, that kea were finally put on trial for sheep killing. For years, High Country farmers had accused them of this heinous deed. Farmers had presented as evidence torn wool and deep wounds on the backs of dead and dying sheep, and related accounts of sheep being ridden over bluffs by up to five kea clinging to their backs. Though most of the evidence was circumstantial, High Country farmers, with assistance from county councils and government, put a bounty of 10 shillings on a kea's head. Within 70 years 150,000 birds had been slaughtered under the scheme. Even if kea were guilty, the sins of a few had been laid at the feet and beaks of all. From 1970 onwards the mountain parrot began to receive protection, yet the jury was still out. The defendant had been neither acquitted nor convicted of the crime of killing sheep. A verdict was finally arrived at in the early 1990s.

At 3.00 a.m., 6,000 feet up a mountain in the depths of winter, no creature should be active, yet it was then and there that the kea struck. A small flock of merinos was camped for the night close to a large rock. This is also where video cameraman Paul Donovan and documentary producer Rod Morris had set up their infrared lights. These "black" lights were invisible to all eyes except the monocular stare of the camera. A sudden movement among the resting sheep first signalled the attack. Then the small, silver retinas of kea eyes could be seen gleaming in the dark. In silence and with stealth, the murderers stalked their victim. Quickly they were on its back, digging into the wool, opening the skin above the kidneys close to the spine with a surgeon's skill. Then they took turns to slurp noisily at the warm blood that welled up into the wound. Meanwhile the merino could only try to exorcise its pain by walking; it was quite incapable of dislodging its ghoulish jockeys.

There it was. Proof. Kea were guilty of sheep killing, and had been for over 100 years. Their latest victim would die a few days later.

Kea may be guilty, but is their misdeed really such a crime? Do they not claim some proprietary rights to these mountains, which they have occupied through several ice ages since the mountains themselves began to rise? Kea take food wherever they can find it. They consume more than 100 plant and animal items in their perpetual search for High Country sustenance. The blood and flesh of sheep are just one food source, consumed by some few "rogue" kea and a number of easily lead youngsters that have developed the taste.

One reason why kea attack sheep is to be found 400 kilometres to the north of Glenorchy. On summer nights the snowy slopes of the Seaward Kaikoura mountains are bathed in sparkling moonlight and echo to the insomniac sighs and coos from the burrows of nesting Hutton's shearwaters, sea birds the size of pigeons. There are visitors in the colony. Gentle calls turn to shrieks as a determined head with a hooked beak is suddenly thrust into a subterranean nest chamber. Despite vigorous protest from the shearwaters, the visitor withdraws clasping their helpless fluffy offspring. Out on the snow the kea then tears open the skin that covers the breast of the still warm chick and scrapes hungrily at the subcutaneous fat. That is all it takes. Around the colony lie several other victims, similarly defiled. The chicks' remains will provide breakfast for harrier hawks and other carrion feeders.

Both incidents of predation, the one in Otago and the other at Kaikoura, could be linked by the kea's need for fat. Research indicates that all parrots, be they tropical macaws or alpine kea, have a requirement to increase fat uptake as a prelude to breeding by between 30 and 60 per cent. As a rule parrots do this by targeting seeds and other sources of plant fats. The kea alone has developed a taste for the fat of animals. This preference could have grown from convenience, accident, necessity or perhaps all three. The kea's vegetarian intake of leaves, snowberries and seeds provides some plant lipid, but is it sufficient for its needs?

The flames of burning refuse at the Arthurs Pass rubbish tip dance in the eyes of young kea. Their fascination with this new phenomenon is so powerful that they boldly walk forward to taste the flames. It is here that the kea's passion for fat, which verges on an obsession, can be observed. A young kea with singed face feathers retires in pain to watch its parents feed among the scraps.

A curious kea looks on at an alpine ski field. Each year these unusual mountain parrots cause damage to vehicles and property as they examine everything with interest. Feeding the birds does little to solve the problem.

Observation and imitation are safer ways of learning what is food and what is not. Another youngster brazenly steals food from an adult's beak. This type of robbery or klepto-parasitism is tolerated as part of learning about the right food.

There are some food items, however, that are so precious to an adult kea that they are taken away to be eaten in solitude. One bird, with a cardboard container in its beak, flies over to hide among the beech trees nearby. Here it uses both foot and bill to effortlessly prise open a tetrapac yoghurt carton. It greedily devours the remaining drops of premium liquid and then casts the package aside. Littered about the forest floor are many such containers similarly discarded by other clandestine consumers. Labels and packaging may be different but what they share is similar content. All these secret kea feasts were of foods that contain dairy products. Cheese, cottage cheese, sour cream, butter, yoghurt, ice cream and milk are fatty treasures to be consumed away from prying eyes. Too much fat is probably as bad for kea as it is for us. In moderation, however, animal fat gleaned from our discards at ski fields, mountain huts and alpine refuse tips, being extremely high in energy, is high also in survival value for mountain parrots.

It is intriguing to consider that long before humans brought fatty fast food to the mountains kea perhaps visited their own regular outlets. Such places could have been found around the edges of the many shallow swamps on the eastern side of the South Island. Bones unearthed at the now famous Pyramid Valley swamp in Canterbury are of course largely those of moa. The bogs in this area held a fatal attraction for several species of heavy-footed moa, particularly in the dry summer months. It is presumed that many of these animals became bogged and lost their lives while crossing the muddy swamp in search of a drink of water. Some bones, however, tell of different swamp dwellers; geese, swans and pelicans, together with other birds known and unknown, visited here. So did their predators, of which *Harpagornis*, the giant eagle, was the most obvious and the most feared.

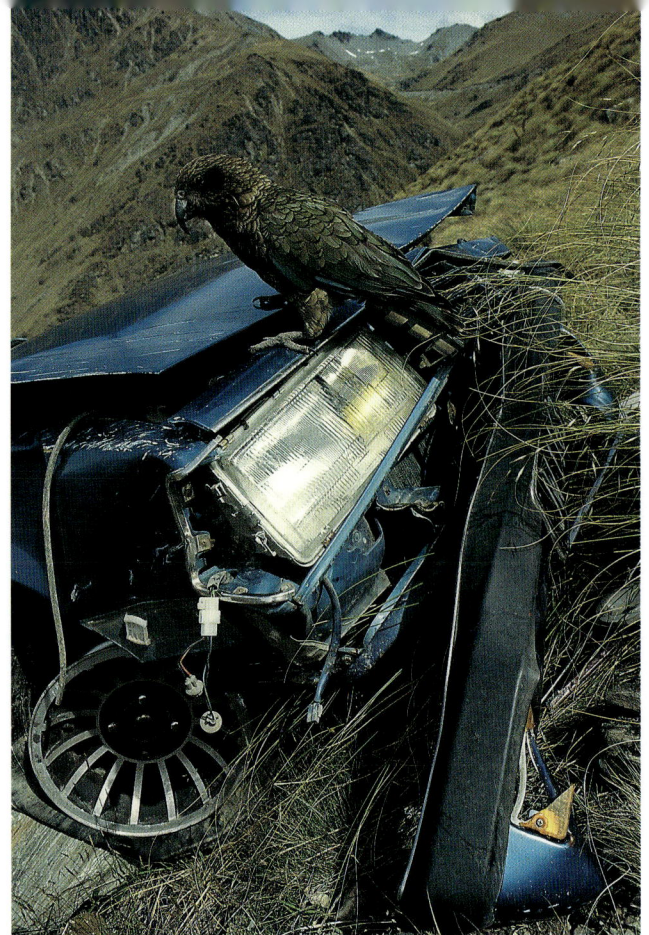

On the broad, flat pelvic bone of several large moa can clearly be seen holes that match, in size and spread, the vice-like clamp of giant eagle talons. This was the point of attack. Once immobilised, a moa was probably killed by blood loss through openings torn in its back and flanks. Other, smaller pelvises show the beak holes of smaller attackers. Does the presence of a generous number of kea bones in several lowland swamps indicate that these holes were made by the "mountain" parrot? There is no reason to think not. Perhaps kea were riding the backs of large feathered herbivores, and attacking and killing them, long before the woolly variety came to these shores. Did moa supply some parrots with their requirement of fat long before dairy products were available? It is difficult to know how far kea once roamed. Their present range, like that of much of our wildlife, is likely to be but a fraction of their former dominion.

A pair of young kea play-fight exuberantly in the snow. They reverse roles regularly, defender becoming attacker, just like children armed with wooden swords or plastic machine guns. Play is just one of the unusual behaviour traits of young mountain parrots. Like human infants, and unlike most other birds, young kea have what can only be described as a childhood. After hatching they spend six weeks in the nest, followed by a couple of flightless weeks close by. First they learn to operate their long, curved beaks and gripping feet. Then they learn to fly, before accompanying their parents for several more weeks learning the ways of the mountains of South Island New Zealand. Nothing escapes their keen eyes; everything, until proved otherwise, is food.

It is after they have left their parents but are still young and inexperienced that some kea get into mischief. These are often the thieves, acrobats, vandals and clowns we see around ski fields. These are the kea that, in some areas, are led on to become sheep killers. But we must forge a new relationship with the kea. Even though some are guilty as charged of the crime of sheep killing, most live very private lives away from human activities. The term "killer clown" should not be used as the title of a modern propaganda campaign against all kea, but as a celebration of one of the most treasured species ever to arise in this land of unique birds. It has grown up with the Southern Alps and survives with resourcefulness and good humour, despite all it has endured as its high country has been "developed".

Above: A juvenile kea removes a milk-shake container from a rubbish bag at the Arthur's Pass tip. Kea visiting the tip target dairy products, the remnants of which they carry off into the surrounding forest to consume in secret rather than share with other kea.

Left: A kea surveys the latest object to be left by people in its mountain home — a wrecked car lying in the tussock on the Remarkables ski field in summer. Such a vehicle will provide hours of entertainment for the mountain parrot, who will test vinyl, rubber and bright chrome with its beak and tongue.

Free of the confines of the nest at last, two young kea celebrate their liberty in boisterous play. Hopping and flapping serves to strengthen young wings and to enhance coordination, but play is also considered a sign of intelligence in juvenile animals.

Kea from the Seaward Kaikoura mountains have learnt to break and eat shearwater eggs raided from burrows by throwing them to the ground (*above left and centre*). Later in the season, the same kea dig up and kill Hutton's shearwater chicks (*above right and right*), but eat only the sub-cutaneous fat, leaving the rest of the carcass for daytime scavengers such as harrier hawks.

Centre right: A young mountain parrot examines the bloodied carcass of a culled red deer.

Far right: Caught in the act: two kea with a merino wether they have attacked in the snow. This extraordinary photograph is visual confirmation of High Country stories which have circulated for years, telling of attacks by the mountain parrot on live sheep.

A female kea tenderly feeds her newly hatched chick (*top left*). Less than a day old, the youngster will be two months in the nest. At six weeks (*left*), it begins to shed its down, exposing the feathers beneath. The chick's yellow facial wattles serve as a resting pad for the female's sharp-tipped beak at feeding time. Young kea begin to emerge from the nest a fortnight later and explore their surroundings. Outside the nest entrance (*above*), a female feeds her two offspring, who are still unable to fly.

UNLIKELY PREDATORS

CHAPTER ELEVEN

JUST OFF AN INTERNATIONAL FLIGHT FIGHTING JET LAG, they head away by the coachload. All have come to see predators, and the more the better. Travel brochures tell of many thousands of the beasts. But can you believe them? Finally, excitedly, they reach the cathedral of carnage — Waitomo Caves.

Pay the money, down the steps into a vast limestone cavern, all aboard the boat and float into darkness — but not for long. It's as if a vast, black cloud slides slowly away to reveal an astonishing subterranean night sky of twinkling stars. A few boatmates exhale a whispered "Oooh". The galaxies at Waitomo never fail to impress, and visitors are usually aware of what they are being impressed by. The stars in the heavens of these caves twinkle from the nether regions of predatory larvae called glow-worms.

Glow-worms cunningly produce their lights by slow burning a waste product called luciferin. Cool combustion takes place in the presence of a specific enzyme and requires chemical energy plus oxygen. This whole remarkable process occurs within an organ close to the larva's rear end. The purpose of the glow is to attract flying prey from the dark, in much the same way that the lights on the decks of squid boats attract squid up from the black depths of the ocean. Each glow-worm dangles up to 70 sticky, silken fishing lines to catch whatever may fly up to its light. Like lazy anglers, the glow-worms lie glowing in their silken hammocks, waiting for a mosquito, moth or other flying insect to twitch their dangling lines! A catch is quickly hauled up and eaten.

Limestone has such properties that it may be shaped and carved over time by the gentle hand of water. However, as visitors to caves close to Nelson stand and marvel at the beautiful and ornate creations of hollowed and precipitated limestone, they are quite unaware of a predator that lurks just above their heads. It is probably best they remain so, because the Nelson cave spider is the biggest arachnid to be found in New Zealand. Its body and legs span an adult human hand. Not that there is any need for panic, as cave spiders hunt cave weta and pose no threat to human beings. They use

Beneath a forest bank a glow-worm rests by day in its silken hammock surrounded by sticky threads.

neither snares nor webs; instead, they feel for the vibrations of an approaching weta in the darkness of the cave. Predators generally do not advertise their presence. They are skilled at concealment, stealth and surprise.

Being predators ourselves we have an interest in others that indulge in the same practice. Lion kills and shark frenzies hold a morbid fascination for us, but some of the most gruesome and bloody encounters take place generally out of sight and between creatures we would not remotely consider capable of being killers.

Every day the wind scatters many tonnes of aged leaves down onto the forest floor. To legions of decomposers this is manna from heaven, which they turn back into soil. To battalions of herbivores it is the stuff of life. To platoons of predators it is the medium in which they hunt the herbivores. The most numerous predators are spiders, harvestmen and pseudoscorpions. Although these eight-legged shock troops snare and pounce on springtails, mites, amphipods and millipedes, they must be careful. Among the leaves another predator is hunting them.

THE VELVET KILLER   The creature has little use for its simple eyes while hunting. Its vivid purple, velvety body bristles with minute, wart-like sensors which have already detected the spider. Fifteen pairs of short legs move the animal forwards, slowly. A pause. The spider moves again, this time — accidentally — within range. The predator has already stretched its body like a small snake. Now it rears up and fires twin jets of liquid glue directly at its prey. The spider struggles but within moments the glue begins to set into strands of rope that bind it more firmly the more it fights. The velvet killer approaches the inert spider in order to pierce its body cavity. Again it stretches out, only this time to contract suddenly, like a syringe, to pump digestive juice into the tightly bound spider. Within a surprisingly short time the juice has done its work and this unlikely predator, a 30-millimetre-long caterpillar-like creature called *Peripatoides novaezealandiae*, is able to drink its prey.

179

The various peripatus species are members of an impossibly ancient group of animals which has existed since the middle of the Cambrian period 500 million years ago. This sort of lineage puts peripatus among the first creatures to live a life on the dry land of this planet. A peripatus has a very close attachment to its piece of forest and may be found, years after the trees have gone, still living and hunting under rotten logs in the middle of a grassy field.

SLIME CRIMES   Snails are surely the unlikeliest of predators. These are not vegetarian garden bandits but forest hunters that pursue their dinner deep within the leaf litter. Slow they may be, but the worms they chase are slower still. The New Zealand gastropod (literally "stomach foot") land speed record is held by the northern kauri snail, which uses a top speed of just over 1 metre per minute to run down its invertebrate prey.

On damp, dark nights, kauri snails emerge to go hunting. The eyes on their antennae are of little use except for light detection. To hunt they use their well-honed sense of smell. Kauri snails have been observed to rear up and pounce on their victims; then, like some slimy wrestler, the snail pins down its wriggling opponent which, once subdued, it proceeds to eat alive.

To Maori the kauri snail is pupurangi — the snail of the sky. It is held in respect for its ability to climb trees and reside close to the stars. It is a mammoth undertaking for a snail, with a shell the size of a matchbox, to climb 20 metres into the branches of a kauri tree, but once up there the hunting is excellent. The leaf litter of tree-perching *Collospermum* and other plants forms gardens of invertebrate-rich humus in the crotch of giant kauri branches.

The unlikeliest of this group of unlikely predators must be the gastronomically deviant members of a primitive genus of light-brown, crinkly shelled snails called *Rhytida*. Cannibalism is by no means unusual among snails, but the *Rhytida* species' method of dispatching their own kind is unique. First one snail fronts up to another and literally bites its head off. That is just the appetizer, but the main course is now inaccessibly constrained within the dead snail's shell. What happens next is a remarkable act of "heads or tails". The cannibal snail lengthens its tail and attaches it to the shell of its victim, which it then drags away, like a tow truck with a smashed car, back to a suitable hiding place. Once concealed, the killer goes to work on the dead snail. Again it lengthens its tail, but this time inserts it corkscrew-like inside the shell to mash up its victim's body organs. The predator then eats, or drinks, its meal at leisure.

This whole process may take several days, and was first observed by the unbelieving eyes of ecologist Dr Murray Efford, who thought it was a freak event. He has now conducted experiments to show that all species of *Rhytida* are disposed to this unlikely behaviour, which is now used as one basis of identification and taxonomy.

Land snails have flourished in New Zealand as nowhere else in the world. There are well over 500 species, which is surprising given that snails evolve at a rate complementary to the speed at which

Left: A carnivorous kauri snail hunts its prey in the leaf litter of a Northland kauri forest. Unlike most of New Zealand's other giant land snails, kauri snails are excellent climbers and can hunt high in the trees.
Above: A woodformed giant land snail examines an empty shell on the mossy forest floor of Karamea Hill, north Westland. Isolated populations of other large snails on surrounding peaks are characterised by different shell markings and colours.

they do everything else — very, very slowly. Snail superiority is due in part to New Zealand's long isolation without mammalian predators and was possibly assisted by the relative absence of snails' old competitors, the ants. There are snails of many shapes, sizes and affectations. Some smaller shells are festooned with spikes as an anti-predator (probably anti-cannibal) device. The smallest shells fit through the eye of a needle, whereas the largest, fully 100 millimetres across, fill the palm of one's hand.

The largest snails belong to the genus *Powelliphanta* (named after Auckland Museum snail expert A.W.B. Powell). These are living works of art. Each species features a distinctively coloured shell, which may be of burnished gold or patterned with stripes like the grain in a piece of highly polished wood. *Powelliphanta* is best known from the several species that inhabit the hilltop forests of the northwest South Island. These hunt worms in deep leaf litter and eat them alive like spaghetti. Two powelliphantids have been observed, like lovers in an Italian restaurant, feeding from opposite ends of the same worm. It took more than a day for the two finally to come together in wormless union. It has been suggested that hungry powelliphantids release a chemical into their mucus which acts to immobilise worms that come in contact with it. When snails are not hungry, worms move across their mucus trails without the slightest effect.

ISLAND ODDBALLS   Although individual species may be represented in great numbers on offshore islands, there tend to be fewer species overall than on the mainland, therefore island ecosystems are often much simpler. One effect of this is that island predators tend to experiment with new, often unlikely roles.

The Poor Knights Islands, northeast of Whangarei, are a stage for several surprise acts of carnivorousness, particularly at night. Up above in the canopy of pohutukawa the flowers are pollinated not by birds and bees but by several species of lizard. Down below in the leaf litter things get even weirder. A purple shore crab clutches at the shell of a large flax snail. The crab purposefully drags the thick-shelled, vegetarian snail back towards its rock pool, which is some hundreds of metres away through the forest. True land crabs are a common feature of tropical lands, but temperate shore crabs wandering through a forest of pohutukawa and ngaio is downright peculiar.

The marathon journey ends when the crab finally returns to its medium of survival, the saltwater rock pool. Here, on underwater ledges and in crevices, lie the discarded shells of many other flax snails brought here previously. Upon immersion the latest victim emerges from its shell in panic and is swiftly butchered by the hungry crab.

It is generally assumed, by us vertebrates at least, that animals with backbones will win any battle against those without. But what happens when an invertebrate reaches a great size? On the Poor Knights a feisty, 15-centimetre-long centipede hunts the leaf litter for a variety of prey, usually of an invertebrate nature like itself. However, when opportunity presents itself it will take animals that are above its evolutionarily modest station. Pausing near a small gecko as long as itself, the centipede lashes sideways, plunging its fangs into the body of the hapless lizard. In the struggle that ensues, the predator maintains its firm grasp while poison slowly drips into its victim and paralyses it. Before the night is over, the lizard will be reduced to a bare skeleton.

The success of the unlikely predators of mainland New Zealand and offshore islands such as the Poor Knights attests to the victory of opportunity and killing power over size and evolutionary status. In all cases it has been the condition of long isolation and freedom from continental predators that has granted species the opportunity to step into new roles. Where predators have been few, new ones have been recruited from unlikely places — from the sea in the case of the forest-roaming crab, and from among traditional prey animals in the case of the lizard-eating centipede. On islands the boundaries of acceptable behaviour can alter and shift such that the unlikeliest of animals are able to experiment not just in the rather specialised art of predation but also in virtually every other niche or role that is available. Incredible things happen on islands, and in New Zealand, a fragment of continent cut off island-like for the longest time of any landmass on earth, the incredible has become commonplace.

The plants and animals of New Zealand have been free to experiment in function and design in ways that have been impossible in other parts of the world. When continental predators finally came to these shores, not only did they quickly and systematically destroy many of the experiments but the laboratory itself was never to be the same again. Though it has been said many times, rather like a message on an endless tape loop which, through constant repetition, loses its meaning, it is nevertheless true that the only guarantee of survival for many of our highly original and often unlikely living treasures is the protective isolation of predator-free offshore islands. Here the bold evolutionary experiments can at least be preserved, and New Zealand's unique life forms, which have been described as the closest thing we will know to life on another planet, can endure.

Some unlikely predators are only safe on rat-free islands such as the Poor Knights.
Above left: A purple shore crab a long way from its rock-pool home drags a flax snail across the forest floor on its way back to the seashore, where it will drown the snail and eat it.
Above right: A giant centipede paralyses a common gecko, as large as itself, on the forest floor before devouring it.

Above left: Two peripatus hunt through the moist rotten wood of a totara log for spiders and other invertebrates.

Above right: Scarcely more than a millimetre long, a tiny pseudo-scorpion (a relative of real scorpions but without a stinging tail) terrorises small invertebrates in the forest leaf litter.

Right: On a cave ceiling, a Nelson cave spider lies in wait for its cave weta prey, whose presence it senses through its long, fine legs.

Far right: The predatory larva of a fungus gnat, a New Zealand glow-worm, lies in its silken hammock waiting for insect prey to fly into the sticky threads.

Once hunted by collectors for their burnished shells, *Powelliphanta* land snails occur in nearly 30 different varieties in New Zealand, distinguished from each other by shell colour and pattern. All are carnivorous hunters of forest earthworms. Travers' giant land snail (*far left*) hunts in the lower North Island. Many other species are concentrated in the top northwest corner of the South Island. Hochstetter's giant land snail (*left*) comes from Takaka Hill. Another (*above left*) comes from near the Oparara River, and the superb giant land snail (*above right*) comes from the Heaphy River area. These last two are among the largest of our land snails, with shells that can span the palm of a man's hand.

Below: The majority of New Zealand's land snails are minute creatures with ornate, decorated shells 1 to 1.5 millimetres across. This masterpiece on moss is covered in fine bristles, possibly to safeguard against being engulfed by larger snails.

Danger of a very different kind has claimed the life of the *Porina* caterpillar (*above*). While feeding underground it has ingested the spores of a fungus, which has taken over its body. The spear-like fungus now scatters its spores over the forest floor, ready for the next generation of caterpillars.

Right: Nutrients of all kinds fall to the forest floor. Among the decaying leaves lies a white-capped noddy and her chick, victims of an unlikely plant predator. The sticky seed clusters of the *Pisonia* tree cling to the plumage of tree-nesting sea birds as an aid to seed dispersal, but in good seeding years the seeds become such a heavy burden to the birds that their plumage becomes "glued" and they fall, weak and dying, to the ground. Here their bodies provide nutrients for the tree that has killed them as well as for passing scavengers.

INDEX